SPIRITUAL HEALING

SPIRITUAL HEALING

The Surrender that Brings Victory

CHERYL GNAGEY

DESTINY IMAGE® PUBLISHERS, INC.

P.O. Box 310, Shippensburg, PA 17257-0310

"Speaking to the Purposes of God for This Generation and for the Generations to Come."

This book and all other Destiny Image, Revival Press, MercyPlace, Fresh Bread, Destiny Image Fiction, and Treasure House books are available at Christian bookstores and distributors worldwide.

For a U.S. bookstore nearest you, call 1-800-722-6774.

For more information on foreign distributors, call 717-532-3040.

Reach us on the Internet: www.destinyimage.com.

ISBN 13 TP: 978-0-7684-3761-4

ISBN 13 Ebook: 978-0-7684-9002-2

For Worldwide Distribution, Printed in the U.S.A.

1 2 3 4 5 6 /14 13 12 11

DEDICATION

This book is dedicated to my Lord and Savior Jesus Christ. I surrender to You all the glory and honor, for without Your constant urging, I would never have completed the task. Thank You for opening up so great a door of adventure and faith that taught me to simply be a vessel through whom You could work. Thank You for showing me so completely the meaning of blind faith and its importance in my daily walk. You have grown my faith by giving me the impossible to do, causing me to utterly rely solely on You.

I also dedicate this book to my loving and supportive husband and best friend, Nevin. You have been my biggest fan and encourager, the one who held me close through my own journey of seeing my broken heart restored, and who challenged me with wild excitement to become everything that God desires for me to be. You are the wind beneath *my* wings. Oh, how I love you, sweetie.

Finally, to those whose hearts are wounded and bleeding...

To those who search for more of Jesus and less of themselves in their Christian journey...

To those who know that there is a surrender that they have not yet experienced...

To those who long to walk in the Spirit and leave their flesh behind...

To every believer whose heart has been torn by painful events or by the bondage to sin that holds you captive in continual spiritual failure and that keeps you from the victory that you know is possible...

To you I also dedicate this book, praying that within its pages you will discover that it is Jesus, and Him alone, who is the Restorer and Healer of your broken hearts.

ACKNOWLEDGMENTS

I have been incredibly blessed to have been surrounded by a number of people who have supported me and held my arms up during this quest. They have been the ones who have encouraged me by what they could "see" in me that, to me, was sometimes elusive. They have willingly shared their gifts with me, doing whatever it took to urge me on in this unfamiliar territory. My heartfelt and loving thanks to:

Berton Heleine, who was the first one to plant the seed that I would surely write a book. Your seed is now coming into full bloom.

Fred Yawn, who never ceased to ask how the book was coming along. You challenged me, sometimes with a swift kick, to push forward. You were the nutrient-rich soil that fed the seed.

Marti Statler, who was a breath of fresh air to this newbie to the publishing industry. You have been a delight and joy to me as you walked me through the first stages of publishing. You were the soft spring rain that has given refreshment to my soul.

And to my personal editing team that helped me prepare this manuscript for submission:

Karen Mitchell, who diligently searched for grammatical and punctuation errors.

Ted Mitchell, who always had the best *excellent* words to replace my *good* words.

Andrea Kukura, who never hesitated to seek clarification so that all would understand.

Larry Gnagey (my father-in-law), who called me back to my "good English."

And Nevin Gnagey (my husband), who constantly put my thoughts into proper order.

You all were the much-needed sunshine that helped the seed grow up into this blossoming flower.

All of you were so necessary for the seed to become a growing plant that would bear fruit. I'll be watching for the great spiritual harvest. It is your fruit, too. Thank you for joining me on this journey. I am forever grateful for you, for your input, and for the God I see in you.

ENDORSEMENTS

What a powerful, challenging book Cheryl Gnagey has given us in *Spiritual Healing*. She brings us face to face with a total allegiance of our lives to God. Through her golden chain of Scriptures, she shows us how to live in the presence of God in an intimacy many believers never experience. As a pastor, I would encourage all believers to read *Spiritual Healing* for their spiritual victory over sin and the building of the church of Jesus Christ. Believers who read this book will strengthen the Body of Christ and make the efforts of every pastor much more fruitful. A congregation that has given themselves totally to the power and control of God will have a greater passion for souls and for service.

Cheryl has pointed out to us the great truth that Jesus' death upon the cross actually broke the yoke of sin visited upon mankind from the sin of Adam and Eve. Today, through Christ's finished work upon the cross and by the power of the Holy Spirit, believers wearing the whole armor of God come into a new lifestyle that brings glory to His name! We are able to live in a spiritual victory through our total surrender to the perfect will of God.

Dr. Berton Heleine
Pastor, Cornerstone Community Church
President Emeritus, American Evangelical Christian University
Treasurer, American Evangelical Christian University
Member of the Board of Regents, American Evangelical Christian University

I was so refreshed by the common sense style in which Cheryl Gnagey has written *Spiritual Healing* that I have sought her permission to use it as a textbook in our Master of Arts in Christian Counseling program. This will have a tremendous impact on those whose main focus is the study and application of the Word. She gives tremendous insight into how deeply God loves us, as well as providing excellent examples of how to have a deeper and a more spiritually rewarding relationship with our Lord and how to share that relationship with others.

Rev. Dr. Gordon N. Elliott
President, American Evangelical Christian University
Board of Directors, American Evangelical Christian Churches

As the pastor of a small church, I have to change hats and juggle jobs often. "Keeping all the balls in the air" can be quite a daunting task at times. Shepherds of small flocks know that the Word of God must be central in our preaching and teaching, and often we feel fairly well-prepared in those areas.

For many of us, however, the counseling room is quite another story. Again, we know the Word must be the foundation of our godly counsel to struggling and hurting parishioners, but all too often we get in over our heads. We feel undertrained, overburdened, ill-prepared, and without focus as we muddle through a process of healing. That is where *Spiritual Healing: The Surrender That Brings Victory* enters the picture. This book is based on the rock-solid foundation of God's Word, and it offers a *practical plan* to help a counselee identify heart issues that need change and take action *to let God do the changing*.

The diagram of the heart, when prayed over and thoughtfully utilized, is a springboard for pastoral counselors to identify areas that need to be discussed in light of Scripture and surrendered to God. And Cheryl reminds us continually in her book that there is an outcome in this process that matters: *surrender yields spiritual freedom*. And after all, isn't *freedom* the goal of spiritual counseling?

I may be a little biased, since Cheryl Gnagey is my wife. But I also know her better than most (if not all) of you who will read this book and experience the healing that is available to you. This concept has radically changed Cheryl's life, and the Lord has led her to share it with you. Cheryl's heart is set on God, her motive to share this truth is pure, and her book is *practical*. It should be in the hands and on the shelf of every small church pastor.

Nevin Gnagey, Pastor
Grace Community Church
Jonesboro, Arkansas

If moving from knowledge of God to intimacy with Him is something that you have always desired but rarely experienced, then *Spiritual Healing* is the book for you. This practical and engaging work reveals that finding inner peace is not something hidden but available to all who are open to accepting God's invitation into a deeper walk with Him. Using the Tabernacle of Israel as a pattern of spiritual growth, this work illuminates biblical principles that lead to a changed heart and new life in Christ. In the tradition of Oswald Chambers and A.W. Tozer, Cheryl Gnagey effectively shows that obedience and God dependency are spiritual disciplines to be embraced rather than resisted if transformation and spiritual maturity are to be obtained. As a Christian therapist, I highly recommend this work and will recommend it to clients who are in search of clarity and healing in their lives.

Jeff T. Cline
LPC Clinical Coordinator, Better Life Counseling Center
Jonesboro, Arkansas

No one can sum up all God is able to accomplish through one solitary life, wholly yielded, adjusted, and obedient to Him.

—D.L. Moody

CONTENTS

SECTION THREE: OUR SURRENDER

INTRODUCTION

Obedience. Ugh! This is not a topic about which we typically like to read. We are not prone to like the list of "dos" and "don'ts." We know that obedience requires something of us. And we also know that disobeying will likely bring some form of discipline from the one we have disobeyed. Obedience is a subject that makes us squirm because we know how far short of the goal we fall every single day. So why have I written a book dealing with a subject with which we seem to struggle so much? Because I struggle with it so much! I know how much I need to be taught in this area of my life. And I assume that you are not much different than me.

At the turbulent age of 15, I gave my heart to Christ. I knew that I was in need of a Savior, so I asked Jesus to come into my heart. He did become my Savior, and I became His child. I imagine that your experience in becoming a Christian varies only in the personal details of your life.

When I became a Christian I began to notice something in me that I had never known before. I recognized my sins for what they were—disobedience to God. But there was something else that became apparent to me. I had a fleshly self-will that operated quite well inside of me, and it often ruled my actions and words. I began to see clearly in my own life what Paul described in Romans 7:14-15,21, which says:

For we know that the Law is spiritual, but I am of flesh, sold into bondage to sin. For what I am doing, I do not understand; for I am not practicing what I would like to do, but I am doing the very thing I hate. . .I find then the principle that evil is present in me, the one who wants to do good.

The more I tried to make the necessary changes in my life so that my actions and words would line up with the Word and will of God, the more I seemed to "practice" my sin. I was caught up in the sin-confess-walk in my flesh-sin cycle that plagued me for too many years.

Just a few years ago I recall telling my husband that I could not think of one sin I had truly overcome by a complete and final turning away brought about by heartfelt repentance. Oh, I had laid some things aside, things that I no longer "practiced" on a daily basis. But these sins always seemed to find ways to rear their ugly heads in me and usually when I assumed that they had been defeated in me. This troubled me greatly. I had no real testimony to share with others on the overcoming power of Jesus Christ by His blood shed for me. I could only testify that He was my Savior from the hell I deserved for my sins. But my testimony could not include that He was Lord of my life and Lord over my flesh that wanted to continue to sin. I was saved. I was baptized. I went to church. I paid my tithe. I faithfully sang in the choir. I was raising my children to know Jesus—even homeschooling them. I also became the wife of a pastor when my husband followed his calling out of broadcast news and into the ministry. I was doing many right and obedient things, but I was not overcoming the sin in my life that was keeping me from the vibrant walk with the Lord that I desired deep in my heart. My disobedience was the stumbling block to the Lord's primary purpose for me—an intimate and obedient relationship with Him. My heart was divided, and I knew what Jesus had to say about a divided heart:

But He knew their thoughts and said to them, "Any kingdom divided against itself is laid waste; and a house divided against itself falls" (Luke 11:17).

As I questioned the Lord about how I might obtain an "undivided" heart, He was utterly faithful to show me several ways to walk in obedience to Him. The Word itself has clarified for me the call of every believer to live an obedient life through the power of the Holy Spirit, given to us for that very purpose. And being a person who learns things much better by sight, God has revealed three major truths to me in visual form. The first is a picture of our hearts as symbolized by the Tabernacle. The second is a picture of our hearts filled with the "gods" that reside there. And the third is a picture of something in the physical realm that He used to teach me a spiritual truth regarding surrender. My prayer is that God will use all three of them to transform your walk with Him, as they have mine.

This book is the result of my journey with God. That journey has led me into His daily presence with a heart that is more and more united and whose divisions are becoming "less and less" as Jesus becomes greater and greater within me.

Spiritual Healing has come about in a very unconventional way. I never set out to write a book. I set out to know how to walk obediently. But as I began that journey, God revealed His plan for this book. Knowing I was a complete novice at writing books, He showed me what to do, one stage at a time, and has proven His point that His "grace is sufficient" for me, and that His power is always perfected through the weakness found in His vessels! Through a word spoken to my heart saying, *You will write a book,* ten minutes of commentary on the Tabernacle of God by a television pastor gifted in the Old Testament, writing some lessons for women's ministry at our church on the topic of obedience, and teaching what I had learned to our small group, this book has come into existence. And to God be all the glory!

My prayer for everyone who reads *Spiritual Healing* is that the God of your heart will lead you into the Holy of Holies, the place of His glorious presence and rest, by uniting your *"heart to fear* [His] *name"* (Ps. 86:11). Then you will experience walking in the very presence of the Lord by the Spirit and in the truth of His Word. This is the process that the Word calls sanctification—the life of Christ (His obedience and holiness) being lived out through His children.

Oswald Chambers asks us this question and challenges us when he says this:

> Am I prepared to let God grip me by His power and do a work in me that is worthy of Himself? Sanctification is not my idea of what I want God to do for me; sanctification is God's idea of what He wants to do for me, and He has to get me into the attitude of mind and spirit where at any cost I will let Him sanctify me wholly.[1]

God has a promise for those who wish to embark on the journey to holiness: *the undivided heart.* He gave the promise to Ezekiel.

> *I will give them an undivided heart and put a new spirit in them; I will remove from them their heart of stone and give them a heart of flesh* (Ezekiel 11:19 NIV).

Are you willing to let God make you "wholly holy"? If you are, then read on. And Godspeed on your journey into the Holy of Holies!

ENDNOTE

1. Oswald Chambers, *My Utmost for His Highest* (Grand Rapids, MI: Discovery House Publishers, 1963), 227.

SECTION ONE

GOD'S TABERNACLE

CHAPTER I

A GLANCE AT THE TABERNACLE

For we are the temple of the living God; just as God said, "I will dwell in them and walk among them; and I will be their God, and they shall be My people" (2 Corinthians 6:16).

In 1982, Kim Linehan won a gold medal in the Women's 800-meter freestyle at the World Championships. The *Texas Monthly* recorded this the previous year: "Kim Linehan holds the world record in the Women's 1500-meter freestyle. According to her coach, Paul Bergen, the 18-year-old is the leading amateur woman distance swimmer in the world. Kim does endless exercises and swims 7 to 12 miles a day. The hardest part of her regimen? 'Getting in the water,' she says."[1]

Simply beginning at the beginning is exactly what we must do if we are to unravel the mysteries of the Wilderness Tabernacle and its crucial meaning to us today. We have to jump into the water of the Word! Don't be overwhelmed, especially if your knowledge of the Old Testament is limited. Simply commit to learn all that you can. You will get it! Are you ready? Are you dangling your toes into the water? Go ahead now. Slip into the water. It might be cold, but you will warm up quickly. Come on now! We have a "big swim" ahead of us!

Our first dip into the water is going to take us back to God's plan for the Israelites, His chosen people. It involves a very interesting tent of meeting that is prophetic for believers in Christ today. Let's begin our walk through the Wilderness Tabernacle.

GOD'S INITIAL PLAN

God had a plan from the very beginning for all those who would be His children. The plan had more than a few steps to prepare us for our arrival at the goal. But primarily He wanted to be close to His children, and like any Father would, He desired His children to be obedient to Him because they loved and trusted Him. He would first start with a few; so He spoke to Abraham, calling him into an obedient lifestyle where he would be the father of an entire nation. Next, Abraham would become the father of many nations. From the eternal past, God planned for His chosen people (the Jews) and everyone else (the Gentiles) to be a part of His family. He would first draw us in to His plan, and then in obedience to His commands, we would respond to Him in love.. So He set out to show us His way to come in, learn obedience, and walk in His glorious presence. God showed Moses the initial plan when the time had come to set up the royal priesthood, the Tabernacle and its furnishings, the law, and the sacrificial system. How could we have known that the Tabernacle of the Old Testament would be the perfect picture of our ever-progressing relationship with Him, our journey to holiness and intimacy with God?

In the days of the Israelites' exodus out of Egypt, God spoke to His servant Moses, telling him how to design the Tabernacle where He would dwell and meet with His people. He gave him the intricate designs of the furnishings for the Tabernacle that the priests would use in their ministry before Him. God wanted to go with the Israelites on their journey to the land He was going to give them. The Tabernacle would be His way of dwelling with them as they moved through the wilderness and into the Promised Land.

The Tabernacle would soon become the center of worship for the Israelites, the focal point of their lives. It was there that God provided a way for their sins to be forgiven through the system of animal sacrifices. Then, once a year, the High Priest would enter the Tabernacle's Holy of Holies and atone for the collective and corporate sins of the Jews. This

Tabernacle was a place of ministry to God, and His plan for the Israelites could clearly be seen in the Tabernacle that He had directed them to build. His plan even included the need for the Tabernacle to be moveable and easily transported; therefore, God could move with them wherever He would lead them.

GOD'S DESIRE

God has always desired a deeply intimate and personal relationship with His people. But do we grasp exactly what God means by an "intimate" relationship? The Israelites' idea of deep intimacy with God was simply believing and knowing that their sins were forgiven through the daily animal sacrifices and through the annual atonement of the blood of the sacrificial lamb. It was all they knew. So certainly that was what intimacy with God was, wasn't it?

As believers in Christ, we ought to examine our own hearts as we consider what intimacy with our God actually is. Have we grown in intimacy with Jesus since our own salvation and baptism? Does our daily walk with God reveal the intimacy and personal relationship that God has always desired from us? Have we stopped short of drawing ever closer to God by simply relying on our salvation and baptism, living as if that is all He requires of us? Is that what we consider an intimate and personal relationship with God to be?

Through the Tabernacle of the Old Testament, God has painted a picture for us of His concept of a growing intimacy in our relationship with Him. While the Israelites may not have completely understood this concept and could only be responsible for the truth they had received at that time, we today can gaze into the Tabernacle of God and see His heart, His purpose, and His plan for us. The Tabernacle's symbolism simply cannot be denied by those who claim to belong to God.

There is an undeniable pattern to the Tabernacle. The logic of God's plan is incredible! He has told us in Hebrews 8:2,5 that the Tabernacle of Moses was a pattern, a copy, and a shadow of the true Tabernacle—Heaven. The pattern of Heaven was shown to Moses when he was on the mountain receiving the Ten Commandments. And God showed Moses how the Tabernacle would resemble Heaven. It was a teaching tool for the Israelites to use to understand Heaven, where their God abided. Likewise, the Tabernacle of Moses has become a teaching tool for us. Our hearts are to mimic the Tabernacle, even as the Tabernacle of Moses' day mimicked Heaven.

THE TABERNACLE OF ISRAEL

Look at the diagram of the Tabernacle. In order to understand its relevance to us, we must first understand its relevance, in detail, to the nation of Israel. So let's begin there.

The Tabernacle

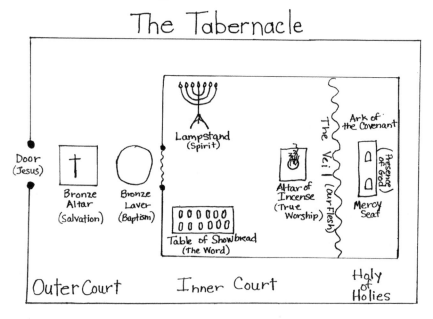

First, let's start with a little Jewish history lesson. God started the human race with just one man, Adam. Adam was created for fellowship with God. God greatly desired to have a relationship with mankind, so God made Adam in His image. Therefore, Adam was created to desire relationships as well. Some 2,000 years later, God made a covenant with Abraham, promising him many descendants and a land for all of them to inhabit. Again, God's desire to fellowship deeply with His creation is seen in the covenant that God initiated with Abraham. From Abraham would come God's chosen people, making Abraham the first patriarch of the Jewish race. His son, Isaac, became the second patriarch, and Isaac's son, Jacob, became the third. It was Jacob who was renamed Israel, thus giving the nation its name. Jacob (Israel) had 12 sons, and each one of them became the head of one of the 12 tribes of Israel.

In the days of Moses, when the Tabernacle was built, the tribe of Levi was chosen to supply the priests who would minister in the Tabernacle. Thus, they became the Levitical priesthood, and their responsibility to the nation of Israel and God was to perform all of the priestly duties that were required by God for the operation of the Tabernacle.

THE SYSTEM OF SACRIFICE

The nation of Israel had been given very clear instructions as to how they were to live their lives before God and within their families. But they were just like us. They had been born into sin because of Adam's sin. Their very humanness made them sin-stained, prideful, and self-centered. So God's plan for the Ten Commandments, the Tabernacle, the sacrificial system, and the priesthood began to show them the sin in their lives. As they sinned and broke the commands of God, they would bring the required sacrifice to the priests, who would then offer the sacrifices up to God. Many of the appropriate sacrifices required were animals whose blood had to be shed on the bronze altar of sacrifice. The blood would be cleansed away from the priests and their utensils in the bronze laver, sometimes called "the sea." When the sacrifice was offered, the person was forgiven of the sin he or she had committed (see Lev. 1:1-13).

All of the priests could offer up the sacrifices, and they ministered in both the outer court and the inner court (sometimes called the Holy Place). But on the Day of Atonement, Yom Kippur, only the High Priest could minister to the people and to God. On this particular day, the High Priest would spiritually prepare all night for his entry into the Holy of Holies by confession of his own sin and the sin of his nation, Israel. Then he would fill the Holy of Holies with the smoke of the incense from the altar of incense just outside the Holy of Holies. Finally, he would sprinkle blood over the Ark of the Covenant, which was the seat of God's mercy. This atonement brought the people into agreement with God for another year (see Lev. 16). But this annual ritual, as well as the countless sacrifices made throughout the year, could never change any of their hearts.

As we begin to investigate what is required of us in order to obtain a changed heart, we must have a fundamental, yet clear, understanding of each part of the Tabernacle as it applied to the nation of Israel. By looking at each court and its furnishings, we will be able to see their importance to us who live now in this Church Age. Look again at the diagram of the Tabernacle.

THE COURTS OF THE TABERNACLE

To the Israelite, the Tabernacle was where God "lived." It was His house, and it was the center of all of their activities. God was obviously present when the smoke of His presence billowed up from the Ark of the Covenant. The door was the only way into the Tabernacle for both the priest and the people. Once inside the Tabernacle, they were standing in the Outer Court. The Inner Court was straight in front of them. Only the priests could go into the rest of the Tabernacle. Once the priests were in the Inner Court, they ministered there, but only the High Priest could enter through the veil and into the Holy of Holies, the place where God's presence and mercy dwelt. The door was the way to forgiveness, worship, and the presence of God.

The altar was the place of sacrifice for the purpose of the forgiveness of sins. The laver was a place of cleansing and ceremonial washings for the priest. The instruments of the sacrifice were also washed there. The bronze altar of sacrifice and the bronze laver were the furnishings of the Outer Court. This Court was the place where the daily sins of the people were taken care of. The people came to the outer court and literally watched their sins being burned up and washed away.

The Inner Court was for the priests alone. It was there that they ministered, not to the people, but to the God they served. In the Inner Court you could find four furnishings. The lamp stand, placed on the south side just inside the Inner Court, was lit continually to bring light into this Holy Place. The table of showbread, placed along the north side, was a symbolic call to God to "show up." It consisted of 12 loaves of unleavened bread that represented the 12 tribes of Israel. New bread was put out on the Sabbath of every week. The altar of incense, placed on the west side just in front of the veil, was a place of continual worship and praise to God. The priest would burn incense and then praise God for who He was; it was not an altar of requests. The veil that separated the Inner Court from the Holy of Holies was a very thick curtain that also separated man from the presence of God.

The Ark of the Covenant, the only furnishing in the Holy of Holies, held the stone tablets on which the Ten Commandments were written, Aaron's rod that had budded (see Numbers 17—Aaron's rod was chosen by God because he was of the household of Levi. Aaron's rod sprouted, put forth buds, produced blossoms, and bore ripe almonds—overnight!), and at one time, a jar of manna from the Israelites' years in the wilderness. The top center of the Ark was called the mercy seat. It was upon this mercy seat, between the wings of the seraphim, that the cloud of God's presence literally dwelt.

THE TABERNACLE'S RELEVANCE TO US

Do you find the Tabernacle interesting? Me too! But just what is God trying to show us today? We are not under the sacrificial system, and no one knows where the Ark of the Covenant is. We only know that it shows up in Heaven in Revelation! Besides, I am not personally of the Jewish race, so what relevance could this possibly have to me, a Gentile? How can we apply something so foreign to us in our Christian lives today?

Again, look at the diagram and see how the Word of God reveals the Tabernacle's meaning to us. Though the picture might seem a little fuzzy at the moment, the Word is about to zoom in and bring the picture into sharp focus for us. Then you will be able to see an amazing picture of God's idea of walking in relationship with Him!

Let's see what insight the Word gives us for the Tabernacle itself. Remember, for the Jews, the Tabernacle was the place where God dwelled with them. Now, see what Ephesians 3:16-17a has to say:

> *That He would grant you, according to the riches of His glory, to be strengthened with power through His Spirit in the inner man, so that Christ may dwell in your hearts through faith. . . .*

Do you see our first connection to the Tabernacle? God once dwelt in the Tabernacle, but He now dwells in the hearts of those who believe in His Son Jesus Christ. Our hearts have become His Tabernacle, His home in us! Awesome, isn't it? The God of all creation has set up residence in the hearts of His children. Now, here is another verse that describes our hearts so well:

> *. . .For we are the temple of the living God; just as God said, "I will dwell in them and walk among them; and I will be their God, and they shall be My people"* (2 Corinthians 6:16).

It is important to know that the temple of God in the days of King David and in the days of Jesus was made in the likeness of the original Tabernacle. It differed in structure and decoration, but not in purpose or layout.

THE OUTER COURT

Let's look into the Word to see what it has to say to us regarding the door of the Tabernacle. This is what Jesus tells us in John 10:9: *"I am the door; if anyone enters through Me, he will be saved. . . ."*

It is amazing that Jesus precisely defines the door in this verse. The door is Jesus Himself! He is the only way into a relationship with God, just as the door of the Tabernacle was also the only entrance into the place where God was.

It is that door that leads us into the Outer Court of the Tabernacle, to the place where the bronze altar of sacrifice and the bronze laver were located. If we look at Luke 22:7 and 23:33, we will see the symbolism of Jesus on the altar of sacrifice.

> *Then came the first day of Unleavened Bread on which the Passover lamb had to be sacrificed.*

> *When they came to the place called The Skull, there they crucified Him and the criminals, one on the right and the other on the left.*

Jesus was the sacrificial Lamb who died for the forgiveness of our sins. His bronze altar was a cruel Roman cross. He was our Atonement. He died, once for all, so that we would never have to pay the price for our sin. He paid the price in full when He was crucified and died on the cross, taking our sin upon Himself. Salvation is the result of believing that Jesus was God's perfect sacrificial Lamb and that He died for us individually and personally.

Following are three verses that shed light on the part the bronze laver plays in our journey to intimacy. Take in the meaning of these verses in light of what you have already learned about the priests and the laver.

> *Having been buried with Him in baptism, in which you were also raised up with Him through faith. . .* (Colossians 2:12).

> *If we confess our sins, He is faithful and righteous to forgive us our sins and to cleanse us from all unrighteousness* (1 John 1:9).

> *Therefore, if anyone cleanses himself from these things, he will be a vessel for honor, sanctified, useful to the Master, prepared for every good work* (2 Timothy 2:21).

After our salvation, we are commanded to be baptized. This action allows us to be identified with Christ, and it is a sign that we have been cleansed by Christ as well. Our salvation and baptism prepare us to "walk in newness of life." Now we are able to be used by God for good works. When we walk forward from our salvation and baptism, we begin the walk toward our full sanctification. Good works go hand in hand with the process of sanctification, being made holy. But at the time of our salvation and baptism, God has merely made us a vessel of honor. Whether we live that out in our lives by holiness will be determined by the choices we make to enter the Inner Court or remain in the Outer Court.

As you look at the diagram again, you can see that these all take place in the Outer Court. We come into a relationship with Jesus, the Door, by our faith in Him. It is our faith that saves us, and we proclaim to the world that we belong to Him when we are publicly baptized into His body. These are all Outer Court experiences. But they are not meant to be the totality of our relationship with Jesus. They are merely the beginning of the journey. We must intentionally and purposefully walk from the Outer Court into the Inner Court. So let's examine next what the Inner Court is all about.

THE INNER COURT

In the Inner Court, the second court of the Tabernacle, the priests carried out their worship to God in the precise way that He had commanded them. For us, it is a place in our journey where we discover very quickly that we are in a "spiritual classroom." It is there that we will discover what true worship really is. By studying the furnishings in the Inner Court, and remembering their significance to the priests, it is not difficult to see that they apply to us on our journey as well. Let's first consider the lamp stand that brought light to the Inner Court. First John 1:7 says:

But if we walk in the Light as He Himself is in the Light, we have fellowship with one another, and the blood of Jesus His Son cleanses us from all sin.

When we walk in the Light, we are walking in the Spirit. He illuminates our way for us as we listen to His voice and obey. He is the One who lives within us. It is His job to sanctify us, making us more and more like Jesus. He is the One whom Jesus promised He would send to us. He is our Helper and our Teacher. Let's also consider that the Old Testament, as well as the New Testament, spoke of Him as our Light. Isaiah 60:1,19-20 tells us this:

Arise, shine, for your light has come; and the glory of the Lord has risen upon you.

For You will have the Lord for an everlasting light (found in both Isaiah 60:19 and 20).

These verses point to the fact that Jesus, who is the Light of the world, could not remain with us. Therefore, the Holy Spirit was given to us at the moment that we were saved, to be our light on this side of eternity. It is in that Holy Place of the Inner Court that we learn to discern the Spirit's voice, learn from Him, and learn to obey Him.

The table of showbread is a picture of the Word of God. God never fails to "show up" when we open the pages of our life's textbook, and map, and moral compass. God is on every page of His Word to us. And in His model prayer for the disciples, Jesus taught them to pray, saying, *"Give us this day our daily bread"* (Matt. 6:11).

The Word is our spiritual food to be taken in and digested for the good of the entire Body. In the Inner Court, we become more than "devotional readers" and casual, sporadic readers who are interested in checking it off of our "to do" lists. Instead, we become students of the Word, seeking to know God Himself through His Word.

Moving on to the altar of incense, we remember that it was a place of worship for the priests. It was a place where they cried out to God, not to gain something from God, but to give something to Him. In the Inner Court, we learn to expand our communication with God from self-centered prayers to praise for who He is. At the altar of worship, we become like the Old Testament priests spoken of in First Chronicles 23:13. We learn to be the fragrant aroma to the Lord, ministering to Him and blessing His name continually.

> *And Aaron was set apart to sanctify him as most holy, he and his sons forever, to burn incense before the Lord, to minister to Him and to bless in His name forever.*

The Inner Court is where great spiritual growth will be experienced at a level high enough that others will be able to detect it in you. In that stage of your journey, you quickly learn that the most important tools for the journey are the Spirit, the Word, and true worship and praise. As we implement these tools, we will eventually find ourselves getting closer and closer to the veil that separates us from the Holy of Holies where God's daily presence can be found.

The veil is what keeps us from the greatest place of intimacy, even though the way has been opened to us since Christ died. So what does the veil symbolize? It actually isn't even a symbol. The Word defines exactly what it is. Consider these two verses:

And behold, the veil of the temple was torn in two from top to bottom... (Matthew 27:51).

Therefore, brethren, since we have confidence to enter the holy place [meaning here is the Holy of Holies] *by the blood of Jesus, by a new and living way which He inaugurated for us through the veil, that is, His flesh* (Hebrews 10:19-20).

It was Jesus' death in the flesh that tore the veil in two. It was not the act of being crucified, or His resurrection, or His ascension into Heaven that opened the way into the Holy of Holies. The veil was torn in two when His flesh died. It died spiritually, as He became obedient even unto death, and physically when He breathed His last. It will be the death of our flesh as well that will rend the veil from top to bottom in our hearts. When we intentionally die to our selfish and fleshly desires by surrendering to God, we gain access to the daily presence of God whereby we can walk in utter obedience. Jesus' death in His flesh made the way available to us, but our flesh will also have to die, as well, in order to step beyond the veil. Paul boldly speaks God's Word this way in Romans 8:12-13:

So then, brethren, we are under obligation, not to the flesh, to live according to the flesh—for if you are living according to the flesh, you must die; but if by the Spirit you are putting to death the deeds of the body, you will live.

The Holy of Holies

The last court in the Tabernacle is the Holy of Holies. The Ark of the Covenant, with its mercy seat, is the only focus of this court. For the Israelites, the Ark of the Covenant was where the very presence of God dwelt, between the wings of the two angels, on the mercy seat. When the High Priest went before the Ark once a year on the Day of Atonement,

God's mercy was poured out on the Israelites. The relevance of the Ark to us today is just as important. When we have walked through the Tabernacle's Outer and Inner Courts with the purpose of being saved and sanctified, our hearts are then prepared to step into the presence of God in His heavenly Tabernacle. Experiencing His manifest presence while we remain in our earthly bodies is possible! In Exodus 40:21, we discover the exact location of the ark in the Tabernacle:

> *He brought the ark into the tabernacle, and set up a veil for the screen, and screened off the ark of the testimony, just as the Lord had commanded Moses.*

Verse 26 clarifies which veil Moses was talking about. It was the veil that separated the Inner Court from the Holy of Holies. In the Inner Court, the altar of incense was just in front of the veil. But on the other side of the veil was the Ark of the Covenant. The High Priest was the only one who was able to experience and witness the presence of God. But every believer who walks through the door to salvation and baptism, and who intentionally enters the Inner Court to allow God to transform his or her heart, will be able to experience that same intimacy in the Holy of Holies if he or she will but crucify his or her own flesh. This is the surrender that brings victory to our spiritual lives!

But what about the mercy seat? How does it pertain to us? In the real Tabernacle of the Israelites, the mercy seat was where the High Priest poured out the blood of the sacrifice for atonement for all the people. Romans 3:25 says, "[Christ Jesus] *whom God displayed publicly as a propitiation in His blood through faith.*" Defined in the Greek, *propitiation* literally means "mercy seat"! Wow! Did you catch that? Jesus' shed blood has figuratively been sprinkled on the mercy seat of our hearts. We can now stand in the presence of a holy God because Jesus is on the mercy seat in Heaven and in our hearts! We can be very intimate with God because of Jesus! Isn't God just incredible and amazing?

THE PROGRESSION OF THE TABERNACLE

As you look again at the diagram of the Tabernacle, do you see with greater clarity the three courts of division? Do you see its progression from the door to the Ark of the Covenant? Have the scales that obstructed your view of Old Testament things been lifted somewhat? Keep in mind that we are working from the premise that the Tabernacle is a picture of our hearts. The furnishings within it reveal the journey we are to make into God's manifest presence once we have walked through the door to salvation. Our salvation leads to baptism; baptism leads to a daily walk in the Spirit, in the Word, and in worship. That true worship will ultimately lead us through the veil and into God's manifest presence. The Tabernacle for us is the picture of the progressive nature of our sanctification; it is from grace to grace.

Defining the Activity of Each Court

Part of what the Lord has shown me about the Tabernacle's relevance to Christian believers is what really happens in our hearts in each court of the Tabernacle. He has shown me how we can clearly define what takes place in each of the courts. As we study each of the three courts, we are going to define in key words what happens there. Those key words will then help you clarify which court you are standing in today. Let's start with some words that will help us see what takes place in our hearts and minds in each of the three courts.

The Outer Court is a picture of the beginning of our walk with Jesus. We believed that Jesus is the Son of God and that He died in place of us for all of our sins. We came through Jesus, the Door, by faith. At that moment, we experienced salvation by receiving Christ, who was the final and necessary sacrifice, who died on an altar called the cross. In obedience to the commandment, we then were baptized into Christ, even as the priests cleansed themselves before serving. This is the start of our journey. Let's call it our introduction to a true faith walk.

Although the Outer Court was our beginning, the Inner Court is the bridge between our salvation and the deepest, most intimate walk we can experience other than eternity with God! Knowing that God never intended for us to stay in the Outer Court, we are to obey the call to walk boldly into God's throne room. In order to get to the throne room of God, we must pass through the Inner Court of Holiness. In the Inner

Court, we learn the importance of a daily walk of obedience. We are taught by the Spirit to walk in the Spirit, and He teaches us truth through our daily reading of the Word. It is in the Inner Court that we learn to worship God in Spirit and in truth. It is the place of illumination for a true faith walk.

Once you have journeyed awhile in the Inner Court and have progressively become more obedient to the Spirit, the Word, and to true worship of God, you will discover yet another phase of your journey. It is what the Tabernacle of your heart has been yearning for since you stepped through the door. It is in the Holy of Holies, God's manifest presence and eternal presence, that you discover it: the intimacy of clinging to God with *all* of your heart, *all* of your soul, *all* of your mind, and *all* of your strength. We were created to love God this way—obediently and intensely!

Are you getting a clearer picture in your spirit about the distinctions of each court of your heart? Let's look at it from one other direction. Do you remember when you first walked through the door? You were a brand-new Christian and had just been baptized. All of your new Christian friends were telling you what you needed to be doing now that you were a member of the family of God...attending church every week, reading your Bible every day, serving in the church in some way, giving your tithe, praying to God. Do you remember being as confused as I was? Where do you begin to read? How do you just "talk" to God? What is a quiet time with God supposed to look like? I clearly remember being overwhelmed, and to my great disadvantage, my pride prevented me from asking too many questions.

I set out to do what I had been told I should be doing. But it was boring to me and too demanding! I didn't understand the Bible very well, and I felt embarrassed speaking to God! I had no desire to spend hours in the Word and with God. I was changed, but not that changed! I struggled along for a while, but I eventually learned that if I was going to read and pray, I would have to discipline myself to "just do it," even if it felt uncomfortable. Disciplining yourself to read might not have been your experience, but all the time that I spent with God in the Outer Court days of my journey eventually came to a close when I began to force myself to draw nearer by way of discipline.

As I got bolder and stronger in the discipline of spending time with God, I eventually began to stick my toe into the Inner Court. I will share in the next chapter the testimony of my experience in the Outer Court. Just suffice it to say, I spent too much time there! I knew that I could have a closer relationship with God than I was experiencing. And I finally figured out that, just like the Levitical priests, I would have to draw physically closer to His presence (by stepping into the Inner Court) if I wanted to be spiritually closer to Him. To be closer to God, I was willing to become even more disciplined in order to achieve that spiritual closeness. I wanted to draw close by stepping closer. After a period of time, I discovered that it was no longer discipline that brought me to my quiet time with my God. It was desire! I was no longer making myself come to Him; I wanted to come to Him! If you haven't come to that place yet, keep disciplining yourself to come. You will soon discover the joy of coming to God out of the great desire of your heart.

Here's another picture that might help you see the difference between the two courts. Have you ever been asked by friends to accompany them to the mall, but you don't have a dime to spend while you are there? You might choose not to go because it wouldn't be any fun at all. Or maybe you decided to go, but your heart just wasn't in it. That is what it is sometimes like in the Outer Court; you go to God out of your personal discipline, but your flesh really doesn't want to be there. On the other hand, a friend might invite you to the mall, and you have Christmas money still waiting to be spent. Excitedly, you go to see what bargains are out there for you! You can't wait to go, because now you desire to be there! Get the picture? Your Inner Court experience will grow into that kind of desire!

But the Holy of Holies elicits an even more extreme response from your spirit. I can honestly say that I have not yet made this the Court of my permanent dwelling, being as yet a student of the Inner Court classroom. On very rare occasions, I have found myself in the presence of God during a quiet time, but it has not yet become the habit of my spiritual journey. When I have found myself in the presence of the Almighty, I have lingered in His presence for awhile because I just had to! And it was pure delight! Does this help you define each court and what happens there? In a moment you will see this even more clearly, especially if you are a "learn by seeing" kind of person, as I am. But first, let me tell you a true story that showed me just what kind of delight we are talking about.

One day in our little storefront church, one of our five-year-olds acted out the principle of the Holy of Holies experience right before my eyes. Josiah was adopted by a family in our church. His young little life had been very difficult. His emotional scars went deep, and he suffered from Fetal Alcohol Syndrome, a very misunderstood malady. But since arriving in his new Christian family, Josiah had shown signs of improvement, slow improvement, but improvement nonetheless. On this particular Sunday, Josiah exited the children's church service to go to the bathroom. He was about to walk right in front of me, as I was seated on the very back wall, when he stopped. There sitting in the back row in front of me was his daddy. You could almost see his thoughts. "Should I go see Daddy? Will that be okay?" Overcoming the questions, Josiah quietly slipped over to where his daddy sat. Without saying a word, Josiah gently reached out his little hand and put it on his daddy's shoulder. Turning, his daddy just smiled at him and placed his big hand on Josiah's. Josiah smiled back with his wide grin, and then he went on with his original plans.

"That's it!" my heart screamed silently. "That's a picture of a heart that wants to enter the presence of God!" You see, when you have walked through the veil of your own dead flesh into the presence of God, and you have enjoyed that intimacy day after day, you just have to go and touch Daddy. Your smiles at each other warm each of your hearts. Daddy's hand on yours makes everything right. Does that make sense? Thanks, Josiah!

Now let's look at the courts with that in mind. Do you see the natural progression of your heart as you grow in relationship with God?

Again, for clarity that needs to seep deep down inside of you, look at the chart below.

THE OUTER COURT	THE INNER COURT	THE HOLY OF HOLIES
Introduction	Illumination	Intimacy
Discipline	Desire	Delight

Okay, is it becoming clearer to you? We will continue to add words to this chart over the next three chapters. This chart will be a helpful tool for you to determine where you are in your journey through the Tabernacle or maybe to help someone else discover where they stand.

THE JOURNEY AHEAD

Didn't God give us a great picture of the Tabernacle of our hearts? If we have this understanding now, what is it that will keep us from walking all the way through the Tabernacle? I don't know about you, but this I know about me: there is only one thing that can keep me out of the Holy of Holies—me! So often I stand in the way of a deeply intimate relationship with my Lord and Savior because I am just too busy or too lazy. I am often more interested in the journey that I have planned, than the one He has. Going into the Holy of Holies will ultimately be up to you; it will be your decision. Access was given to us when the veil was torn from top to bottom the moment Jesus died. He made us part of His royal priesthood. That makes the Tabernacle our *spiritual service of worship* (Rom. 12:1). Will I choose to worship Him appropriately in that way? Will you?

No matter which court you find yourself standing in—the Outer Court (still celebrating your salvation and baptism), the Inner Court (beginning to really develop a deeper relationship with God), or the Holy of Holies (where you delight in being surrendered to Him)—you have room to grow. The goal is to reach the manifest presence of God and stay there, experiencing the level of intimacy and delight that can only be found there. Of course, the final goal is to step through the veil, once and for all, and dwell constantly in the presence of God in Heaven! To dwell intimately in God's presence is a precious gift we can experience both here and in eternity! How much we experience it on earth is in our control. Is that what we desire or not? We know it is what God desires!

God has told us about this amazing entrance into His presence in Hebrews 10:19-25. He says it better than I could ever begin to articulate it. Let Him speak to you as you take a moment to discern which court you are currently standing in and where you want to go:

Therefore, brethren, since we have confidence to enter the holy place by the blood of Jesus, by a new and living way which He inaugurated for us through the veil, that is, His flesh, and since we have a great priest over the house of God, let us draw near with a sincere heart in full assurance of faith, having our hearts sprinkled clean from an evil conscience and our bodies washed with pure water. Let us hold fast the confession of our hope without wavering, for He who promised is faithful; and let us consider how to stimulate one another to love and good deeds, not forsaking our own assembling together, as is the habit of some, but encouraging one another; and all the more as you see the day drawing near.

If your heart is "sprinkled clean" and you have been "washed" in the blood of the Lamb, is it time for you to "draw nearer" to God by entering into the Inner Court? Or is it time for your flesh to die even more in the Inner Court so that you can step through the rent veil into the Holy of Holies? Wherever you stand today, will you make a firm decision to journey deeper into your heart and draw closer to God? God never intended for you to stand in the same place forever, unless you are standing in His daily presence, in the Holy of Holies. God's plan for your heart is clear. He desires for you to make the journey from the door all the way to the Holy of Holies. He does not want you to stay in the Outer Court of your salvation and baptism. There is more! God cries out to you today, saying:

Oh that they had such a heart in them, that they would fear Me and keep all My commandments always, that it may be well with them and with their sons forever! (Deuteronomy 5:29)

THE TABERNACLE IS SET IN OUR HEARTS

Consider with me one more verse that so aptly describes our hearts, God's Tabernacle. Recalling now that the Tabernacle of our hearts takes us from our introduction to Jesus, the Door, all the way to Heaven, where we will stand in God's presence in the Holy of Holies, read this incredible verse: *"He has also set eternity in their heart"* (Eccles. 3:11).

God put the idea of eternity with Him in the heart of every human being! Do you see it? And the Tabernacle of God has been set in the hearts of every believer, for it is a picture of our journey to eternity! To believe in and receive Christ, choosing eternity with Almighty God, is to walk through the door of the Tabernacle now set up in your heart. Have you chosen that for yourself? And does it sadden you, as it does me, to think of how many people have received this eternal Tabernacle set up in their hearts, the Tabernacle of a real and intimate relationship with God, but their Tabernacle is empty and silent because they have refused to walk through the entire Tabernacle? Richard L. Evans conveyed the essence of such procrastinations when he said, "The tragedy of life is not that it ends so soon, but that we wait so long to begin it."[2] As you continue your journey to an unbroken heart, consider praying for those you know who believe in their hearts but are hanging out at the door.

In the next three chapters, we will be peeling away a little more of the mystery of the Tabernacle of our hearts and the picture of our Christian journey that He has set in each one. You've begun a very special journey. Don't stop now. Let's walk through the door together. You are going to love the Outer Court!

INTROSPECTION

1. If the Old Testament Wilderness Tabernacle is a picture of the journey that every Christian's heart is to take, how are the three courts symbolic of that journey?

2. Which word describes your current relationship and experience with God: *discipline* (you have to force yourself to spend time with God), *desire* (you *want* to spend time with God), or

delight (you *have* to spend time with God)? This reveals which court of the Tabernacle you are likely standing in.

3. If the Tabernacle is a map of the journey, it is important to know exactly where you are currently living and where you are to be going. In which court are you standing this very moment?

4. Realizing that the Holy of Holies is the destination for every believer, what step might you take today that would bring you one step closer?

5. With eternity set in your heart, are you ready to walk through the Tabernacle?

ENDNOTES

1. *Texas Monthly*, quoted in *Reader's Digest*, June 1981, www.sermonillustrations.com/a-z/b/beginning.htm.

2. *Bits and Pieces*, (March 4, 1993), 2, www.sermonillustrations.com/a-z/b/beginning.htm.

CHAPTER 2

THE OUTER COURT— THE BEGINNING OF FAITH

I am the way, and the truth, and the life; no one comes to the Father but through Me (John 14:6).

I am the door; if anyone enters through Me, he will be saved... (John 10:9).

Having glanced into the Tabernacle of the Israelites with an eye on how it affects us today, we have seen its general application to us. We have removed the first layer of skin from an onion whose core we desire to see. In this chapter, we will take an "up close and personal" look at the first court of the Tabernacle—the Outer Court. Studying it in detail will allow us to begin to see its importance in our spiritual journey. But before we dig into the meat of the Outer Court, let's do a little review of the entire Tabernacle. It will help us set in stone what we learned in the previous chapter. Here are the first three main points of the Tabernacle's relevance to us.

1. God has always desired a deeply intimate and personal relationship with His children.

2. The Old Testament Tabernacle is a unique picture of the full scope of that relationship between God and His children.

3. Just as the Tabernacle was a place for the Jewish priests to minister to their God and their people, the Tabernacle of our hearts is where we, the royal priesthood of Christ, are to minister to God.

A REVIEW OF THE ENTIRE TABERNACLE

Having laid that foundation, we can now review the parts of the Tabernacle and their symbolic application to our lives. The Tabernacle was a place where God abided and dwelled with the children of Israel. Our hearts are now God's Tabernacle. It is in our hearts that He abides with us through the Spirit given to us at the time of our salvation. The door provided entry for the priests into the Tabernacle. Jesus said He was the Door. We enter into relationship with God through His Son, Jesus. At the moment of salvation, we become a part of His royal priesthood.

The door is the entrance into the Outer Court. In it, the bronze altar was the place of sacrifice for the purpose of forgiveness of sins for the Jew. Jesus' sacrifice and subsequent shed blood gave us the opportunity for salvation. The laver (also Bath or Sea) was a giant tub of water where the priests ceremonially cleansed themselves, as well as the utensils that they used for the animal sacrifices (see 2 Chron. 4:6). Our baptism as believers is our ceremonial "cleansing" that identifies us with Christ, and it is the beginning of our preparation to become a utensil in the hand of God.

In the Inner Court, the lamp stand provided the light. The Holy Spirit is our Light for the journey. The showbread was symbolic of asking God to "show up." The Word is our daily bread in which Jesus always shows up. In the first book of the Bible, bread is tied to the heart. Genesis 18:5 says, *"A piece of bread, that you may refresh yourselves."* Did you know that this literally means "a piece of bread to comfort[1] your hearts"?[2] The altar of incense is where the priests continually worshiped God with praise and offered pleasing aromas to Him. When our praise and worship is focused on God, not our needs, it is true worship and pleases our God. The veil separated unholy man from his holy God. Jesus' crucified flesh opened the way for us to enter the presence of God the moment He died on the cross.

The veil led to the Holy of Holies where God's mercy could be found at the Ark of the Covenant. The law, which represented Israel's covenant relationship with God, was inside the ark. For us, the Ark of the Covenant and the Mercy Seat represent God's constant presence with us. We will experience that to the greatest degree when we enter the gates of Heaven, but we can also experience His presence with us when we present to Him a life of obedience to His Word and the covenant relationship He has offered us.

Hopefully, it has been helpful to you to put the Courts and the furnishings of the Old Testament Tabernacle in context with its relevance for us today. Let the truth of this settle deeply within your heart and mind. God has established all of this for you! He has given it to you to help you more clearly see His plan for your life as a believer.

Now, to be clear as to how all of this relates to our spiritual journeys, we will walk through the Tabernacle one more time.

- Standing outside the door (and the entire Tabernacle) is a representation of those who are not yet saved. They have not walked through the door because they have not yet received Christ as their personal Savior or accepted His sacrifice for their sin.

- Walking through the door represents a belief in Jesus as Savior and the acceptance of His sacrifice on the cross on our behalf, once and for all.

- Standing in the Outer Court is acknowledging that our salvation is in Christ, and the outward sign of our connection to Christ is shown by our baptism.

- Entering into the Inner Court is to participate in the classroom of holy living. It is the bridge between our salvation (the Outer Court) and our future glorification (the Holy of Holies). The classroom will involve the study of the Word, listening to and obeying the voice of the Spirit, and God-focused worship. It is noteworthy that in the Old Testament Tabernacle, an Israelite who was not of the priesthood could come into the Outer Court. But only a priest was allowed to enter into the Inner Court.

- Passing through the veil is to make our way into the presence of God. It can only be accomplished by the death of our will, and a surrender to His. Finding ourselves then in the Holy of Holies, we are able to say that we have undeniably been in the presence of God. This takes place when we reach our eternal home, but it also takes place here on earth, when we walk intimately with Him in full obedience.

Having covered these general aspects of the entire Tabernacle, we are going to focus now and for the rest of this chapter on the details of just the Outer Court. We've walked through the Door of Jesus, and we are now standing in the Outer Court. Pull out your magnifying glass, and let's take a closer look!

A Description of Salvation

We have already identified the furnishings of the Outer Court. They are the altar of sacrifice and the laver. We know that to be standing in this court, we have to have passed through the door of belief, received Jesus' sacrifice for ourselves, and obeyed His command to be baptized. Our individual salvation experiences have been different, but they look like this in some form. You have:

1. Admitted your sinfulness

2. Admitted your need for a Savior

3. Believed Jesus was that Savior

4. Believed that His death on the cross was the power that saved you

5. Asked Him to come into and take up residency in your heart.

To understand the different aspects of the Outer Court, let's add some more descriptive words to our chart from the previous chapter that will bring the Outer Court into clearer focus. Look at the five things listed above. These represent a repentance of the totality of your sin. When you first confessed your sin to Jesus, it was your sin nature that you were confessing. You might have listed several obvious sins in your life as part of your repentance and salvation prayer to Him. But you could not possibly have listed all of your individual sins unless you kept an exhaustive list! And you would not have known what your future sins would be, either! In reality, you confessed that you were of Adam's race and were under the curse of sin. That is why you were repenting. You brought to God a contrite heart that you knew was sinful and a desire to turn away from your disobedient lifestyle and to turn toward Jesus. Believing He could save you from eternal damnation, you gave your spiritually unhealthy heart to Him, asking Him to come and live in you.

I must insert a critical message here. It is easy to make the assumption that everyone who is reading this book is a Christian. It is a pretty safe bet that you are. But if you are reading this and you have never walked through the Door of Jesus and asked Him to be your Savior, that is where you are to begin right now. Return to the five steps of salvation listed earlier. Pray those things from your heart, and truly mean them, and you will be saved. Tell someone that you have asked Jesus to be your Savior. Let that person help you find a church where you can be baptized into the family of God and where you can begin to grow in your relationship with Him.

REVIEWING OUR CHART

As you saw in the first chapter, God has given me helpful "word pictures" to describe what happens in each court of the Tabernacle. So far, He has shown us these:

THE OUTER COURT	THE INNER COURT	THE HOLY OF HOLIES
Introduction	Illumination	Intimacy
Discipline	Desire	Delight

As we move on, I want to add three more sets of words.

Contrite Heart	Change of Heart	Complete Heart
The Way	The Truth	The Life
No fruit or little fruit	More fruit	Much fruit

If these additions are not already giving you goose bumps, they will! It is just amazing how the Scripture illuminates and aligns itself with the Tabernacle! Look at the words again, and then look at your diagram of the Tabernacle. Are you getting the picture?

We've added a contrite heart to the chart under the Outer Court. That is truly what took place at the door of the Tabernacle as you entered into the Outer Court. You came with a contrite heart as you confessed to Jesus your need for Him to save your soul.

Our salvation is to be followed by our baptism into the family of God. It is kind of like an "adoption" ceremony for the Parent and the child! We might not fully realize it at the time, but our baptism into God's family means that we not only identify with God as a child of His, but we also will be required to identify with Jesus in His death and resurrection (see Rom. 6:1-14; Phil. 3:10-11).

THE TEMPORARY STAY IN THE OUTER COURT

Based on the diagram of the Tabernacle, you might then ask yourself if you think that salvation and baptism are all that God has called us to. Do you think He intended for us to stay in the Outer Court of our salvation and baptism? We have a problem in the modern church today. Maybe it was a problem in earlier centuries as well, but it is definitely a problem now! We believers tend to celebrate in the Outer Court, glorying in our salvation, our baptism, our assurance of a spot in Heaven, yet we do not walk in the Spirit. We often claim we do not even know how to do this. We attend church and learn from our pastors and teachers, yet we do not study the manual given to us on our own, claiming to not know how to because it is too difficult to understand. And if we are brutally honest with ourselves, we generally do not have the slightest idea how to truly worship the One we claim to have as our Lord. In our limited understanding, we have reduced "worship" to singing or listening to a few praise songs, when in actuality we worship God by how we live our lives!

If you are a believer who has also been baptized, and you believe that God's children should not remain in the Outer Court forever, it is important for you to know what will be required of you in order to approach and enter the Inner Court.

Look back to our word chart. If you understand that the Outer Court is your introduction into the faith walk, then you can clearly see what will be required of you to approach the Inner Court and enter into your time of illumination. It will require an inner discipline (or determination) to get there. I will be sharing with you my own personal journey into the Inner Court, but for now, simply focus on the fact that spiritual discipline is what it will take for you to arrive at the entrance to the Inner Court.

But let's not run ahead. Look again at the chart. If contrition of our hearts is what occurs as we enter the Outer Court, it is a change of heart that we will experience in the confines of the Inner Court. What I am talking about is the kind of change wherein the Spirit and the Word begin to deal with our individual sins, one at a time. Do you remember the repentance of the totality of our sins that occurred when we were saved? This is a different repentance altogether. This is the repentance where God begins to truly change our hearts by rooting out the individual sins, gods, idols, and attitudes that we serve instead of Him. He will illuminate them for us and work in us until they no longer remain. This is the change of heart to which I refer.

As our hearts begin to change and line up with the Word and will of God in the Inner Court, we will find ourselves drawing very near to the veil. As our flesh dies, and the Spirit is allowed to live out the life of Christ in us to a greater and greater degree, we will find ourselves, on occasion, standing in the very presence of God, experiencing Him like we never have before. This is where we first see our complete heart, a heart that has been matured and perfected within us by the Spirit of God. Now let's add those words to our chart. While we are at it, let's go ahead and complete the chart for this chapter. All of them added together at once will give us a more complete picture of what happens in each court, but particularly in the Outer Court. The final two word sets will be backed up with Scripture, and you will then see what a beautiful picture is being painted for us so that we can understand.

GOD'S WAY

In John 14:6 Jesus tells His disciples, *"I am the way, the truth, and the life; no one comes to the Father but through Me."* Do you see how these terms define Jesus and align with the furnishings of the Tabernacle? Jesus is the Door (see John 10:9), the only Way into the Outer Court, into this relationship that takes place in our hearts. Did you notice that there is no other way into the Tabernacle except through the door? Next, Jesus' Word is complete truth, as He is the Living Word. And where do we find the Word in the Tabernacle? In the Inner Court, of course! And finally, Jesus' presence with us daily and in extraordinary ways is the abundant life promised to us when we "walk as we should," right straight through the Tabernacle.

Now let me ask you a few questions. Have you struggled with whether or not this teaching on the relevance of the Tabernacle to our lives today really lines up with what God intended the Tabernacle to be? Have you thought that this was just stretching the illustration a bit too far? Maybe my third question will answer the first two for you. Is it merely coincidental that Jesus, who was speaking to Thomas about leaving the disciples' presence to prepare a place for them in Heaven, spoke these words in exactly the right order, so that they line up with the pattern of the Tabernacle?

> *I am the way, the truth, and the life; no one comes to the Father but through Me* (John 14:6).

Now, if you really want some hard-core goose bumps, note that Jesus had just given them the answer to where He was going! He said, *"And you know the way where I am going"* (John 14:4). Thomas questions Jesus, saying, *"Lord, we do not know where You are going, how do we know the way?"* (John 14:5).

Jesus answered him by telling him that the way to Heaven could be found by walking through a "Tabernacle" that they were completely familiar with! Jesus said that this walk was the way to where He was going—to Heaven! Do you question the relevance of the Tabernacle in your life anymore? God is utterly precise!

THE VINE AND ITS FRUIT

Looking now at our last set of words, we can even more clearly define the activity in the Outer Court. We will use another passage of Scripture from the Book of John. It is very familiar, I am sure, to most of you. Do you recall the lesson concerning the vine and the branches? Refresh your memory by reading John 15:1-8 several times. What word do you see repeated several times in the eight verses? Did you see that "fruit" might be very important in one of the last messages Jesus gave His disciples just before His death? He mentioned four types of fruit: no fruit, little fruit, more fruit, and much fruit. We have already put them on our chart, but what do they reveal about the courts of the Tabernacle, particularly the Outer Court?

Before we search the verses to answer that question, let's first establish something about the "branches." Who are the branches? Determining this is important in order to understand that those who "bear no fruit" are in the Tabernacle. Could a "branch" be outside of the Tabernacle? I don't believe that the Scriptures back that up. Jesus very clearly states in verse 2 that He is speaking about every branch that is in Him. He says it this way:

> *Every branch in Me that does not bear fruit, He takes away...* (John 15:2).

Do you see that the converse of His statement is also true? There can be no fruit born outside of Him. These four types of fruit of which Jesus speaks are produced through those who are in Him, having come through the Door of the Tabernacle, and who are walking toward the goal of the Holy of Holies, Heaven.

This verse also means that there can be some in Him who don't bear any fruit at all. These are the ones whom *"He takes away."* Jesus says that He will cut off these branches in Him. The Greek definition reads this way: "To take away, remove, with the idea of lifting away from, usually with the idea of violence and authority."[3] We won't go into any more detail on this at this point. But it should cause us to examine our lives to see if we are bearing some amount of fruit. If we are not, it is paramount that we discover how to bear fruit! The responsibility of bearing fruit rests on our shoulders! Do you want to be counted among those who bear no fruit and who are taken away?

For many Christians, the early days in the Outer Court do not include much focus on fruit-bearing. Later, though, in your Outer Court experience you might have been focused on bearing fruit, and if you were, some fruit might have been seen in your life. It is "no fruit and some fruit"[4] that are characteristic of the Outer Court Christian. In order for the Vinedresser, our Father, to produce more fruit through our branches, there is one critical step He takes. He prunes us! Doesn't sound like much fun, does it? No one wants to have their branches cut! But truly, what we think "pruning" means is not what Jesus describes here. Instead it means "to cleanse from filth, to purify."[4] I've never heard this process explained more eloquently, yet simply, than in Bruce Wilkinson's book, *The Secrets of the Vine*. He quotes from a vine-grower from California:

> "New branches have a natural tendency to trail down and grow along the ground. But they don't bear fruit down there. When branches grow along the ground, the leaves get coated in dust. When it rains, they get muddy and mildewed. The branch becomes sick and useless." What would the remedy be for that? Did he cut it off and throw it away? "Oh, no!" he exclaimed. "The branch is much too valuable for that. We go through the vineyard with a bucket of water looking for those branches. We lift them up and wash them off."[5]

In light of this teaching on pruning, can you see that the dirt (sin) on your branch can render you useless and unable to bear fruit? In order for that to change, there has to be a cleansing of the sin in your life in order for you to begin to bear more fruit. That is why moving on from the Outer Court of no fruit and just a little fruit is critical in the life of a

Christian branch! Constant and willful sin cannot remain in the life of a believer if he or she is going to bear more fruit for the Kingdom.

If the Outer Court is where you currently live, you would be wise to take note of any sin God is revealing to you. Let Him lift up your branch, and let Him wash it clean so that you can turn your empty basket or your immature pieces of fruit into the fruit of abundance! Begin to allow the discipline that takes place in the Outer Court, and include the pruning of your known sin. This type of pruning is required before you can enter the Inner Court of the deeper pruning. Don't be a branch that is cut off and taken away because you are not bearing fruit!

To begin to bear more fruit, we must make a choice to abide in the Vine, live in Him, and live for Him. We will be discussing that in the next chapter about the Inner Court. And in the fourth chapter, we will examine how to begin to bear much fruit. In the Inner Court and in the Holy of Holies, we will become very well acquainted with the "pruning" process and will find that we no longer balk at it, but welcome it instead.

It is in the amount of fruit that we are bearing that we will most clearly see in which court we are currently standing. Keep in mind that our goal is to glorify God by stepping into the Holy of Holies. That is where our obedience will bear out much fruit. What do you see in your basket? How full is it? How ripe and mature is the fruit that you see there?

It should be very clear to us by now that God does not intend for us to stay in the comfort and safety of the Outer Court. He wants us to bring glory to His name by a life of baskets and baskets and bushels and bushels of fruit borne out of our desire to obey Him completely. These questions beg to be asked: Do you want to stay where you are, or do you want to step into the Holy of Holies? Are you comfortable running around in the Outer Court, never addressing your sin issues? Are you afraid of what the Spirit might illuminate in your heart? Are you willing to continue the arduous task of hiding your sin from a God who already knows it, a God who desires to wash it away from you? Can you see that what appears painful to you is seen by God as the only way for you to be a branch that brings Him glory?

My Outer Court Experience

No one ever asked these questions of me as I wandered around in the wilderness of my salvation and baptism. Maybe they would have helped me move more quickly from my comfort zone in the Outer Court to the pruning of the Inner Court. As it was, it took me a very long time before I realized my need to move from the playground to the classroom. Here is my story. Use it for insight and the urging to walk forward into the Inner Court. It should not be considered as an example for you to follow.

Growing up in a household where the fruits of alcoholism were abundant, I realized my need for a "covering" long before I understood my need for a Savior. I needed an authority in my life that was good and righteous. I needed someone to help me overcome my obstacles. I wanted to know that I would go to Heaven when I died. So at age 15, at a Lay Witness Mission in a Methodist church in my hometown in Lexington, Illinois, I tearfully gave my life and heart to the One who could save me from the negative effects of growing up in my family. Not long after my salvation, I came to realize that Jesus had saved me from much more than that. He had saved me from all my sins. I was not baptized at that time because I didn't think it applied to me. I had been sprinkled as an infant, and I thought that was all that was required of me.

My high school years were fraught with the same stuff that every teenager was experiencing in the '70s, but I had an understanding of what I shouldn't be doing. That served me well early on, but I did learn to ignore that "little voice in my head." In college I met some really great Christians who displayed an authentic walk in their lives. Until then, I hadn't really known how to walk with Jesus. God began laying the foundation of an intimate relationship with Him for my spiritual journey. I didn't know that I needed more than my salvation. On very rare occasions, I would read a short devotional and be encouraged, but days, weeks, even months would go by without me ever thinking about my daily walk again. I had no understanding that I was wandering around in the Outer Court, basking in my salvation, and that God was setting the course for me to fix my gaze upon the Inner Court. After college, I roomed with a girl who really seemed to know what a Christian should be doing. She was a great example to me, and I gleaned the knowledge of the importance of time spent alone with God from her walk, but that knowledge never really translated into action on my part, let alone a transformed heart and life.

When I got married, it seemed vitally important to me and my husband to get our spiritual lives together, especially in the event that children would follow. We began to do all the things we saw Christians doing. Tithing and regular church attendance became the norm for us, and I even realized my own need to be baptized as an adult. I was privileged to have my husband baptize me. He was a bi-vocational pastor at the time. We branched out into some ministry here and there, but ultimately my ministry fed my own flesh. Instead of igniting a greater desire for God, I desired more ministry. More and more I "served the Lord" by doing all the things I liked to do: music, ladies' Bible studies, fellowshipping. I even began to take exhaustive notes of sermons, to encourage others with the truth, and to be at every event that occurred in our church. I had 10 or 12 very close friends I loved spending time with. We had fun "sharing our burdens together" (otherwise known as gossiping!).

For 25 years, I was perfectly content with my personal relationship with God. I had surely made the right choice in taking Jesus as my Savior. Eternity with Him would be great! But there were a couple of mile markers that showed me now that God wanted more than this for me. The first came after a time of repentant confession. I was challenged by a friend to ask God to fill the void left by what I had confessed with something that would lead me to greater spirituality and growth. What came to mind to ask Him was for a hunger for the Word. I knew that was lacking in me, for sure. So I asked Him to fill the hole created by my recently confessed sin with a true and deep hunger for the Word. He answered my prayer by bringing to me a fun way to study the Bible—Inductive Bible Study—where you dig out the gold for yourself. For several months with only a rare miss, I began to study the Minor Prophets. But I still lacked something that I couldn't quite put my finger on.

What I didn't understand is that for that period of time in my life, while I was wandering around in the Outer Court, I was missing out on personal intimacy with God. I wanted it, but what exactly was it, and how could I get to it? The "it" was the intimacy found in the Inner Court of the Tabernacle that I knew nothing about.

The second marker that catapulted me into the Inner Court was an event orchestrated by God. He definitely drew a line in the sand, and He determined for me that I could no longer walk around in my active church life, thinking that it would suffice in place of a real and intimate walk with Him. The event He allowed in my life was a move from Waterloo, Iowa, to Jonesboro, Arkansas.

You might ask how that could be a catalyst for spiritual change in me. It was a simple plan. God took away my life support systems of church activity and friends. I had learned to turn to them instead of Him, constantly leaving Him behind. He pulled the "religious" carpet right out from underneath my feet. I hit the ground without even knowing what hit me.

Overnight, I was faced with a new reality. I had no friends to depend on, and if you have ever moved before, you know that making new friends is not very easy. These new church people had no history with me. My old friends knew all the Gnagey stories. My new friends knew nothing of me, and they really didn't care about my interesting past. Who would I turn to when I needed someone to talk to? Who would I find fellowship with? What ministries could possibly be as great as my old ones? I was well-established in my ministries, and now I had nothing to do. The start-up church that we would be helping was only 11 months old, with about 60 members. How could that ever "fulfill" a person coming out of a Church of 1,000? And besides, the ministries I wanted to do were already being done by someone else when I arrived.

I felt completely alone as my husband went to work and ministered every day. I was at home, homeschooling our three children, with no friends and no outlets. I was completely isolated and lonely. And to top it off, in the first year, the one friend I felt I had in this new church deeply wounded me and left me out.

That was the point in my life when I made my own line in the sand. From now on, it was going to be a different journey for me—just me and God. I had no one and nothing left to depend upon. This was the last call from God for me to enter the Inner Court that I can recall. I resolved to achieve the goal of intimacy with Him. From that painful moment on, God began to teach me how to have a personal and intimate relationship with Him. I was desperate, so I made the decision to invest first in my time with God, letting everything else come after that.

I am still in the Inner Court with much work left to do. But my time spent daily with the Lord, weeding out my sin, learning to hear more quickly and correctly the voice of the Spirit, and growing in my understanding of worshiping Him in Spirit and truth, has been the most precious time of my journey into the Holy of Holies. And do you know what? I have even had a few experiences of being face to face with God!

That is my story. But I don't want it to be yours. You don't have to wander around in the trappings of the church life. You don't have to wait 25 years to discover what intimacy with God is. You don't have to delay knowing experientially what a deep, intimate, personal relationship with Jesus is because you are in the Outer Court of introduction. You can begin today by disciplining yourself to read your Bible, just a little bit every day. You can ask the Spirit questions about what you read in the Word, and then wait on Him to teach you what you need to know. When you pray, try spending as much time listening to the Spirit as you do talking to Him. After awhile, you will look at your surroundings and discover that you are now standing in the Inner Court of illumination, where it no longer requires discipline to study and pray. It is now out of desire that you come to Him!

Maybe this checklist will help you get going!

1. Write down what commitment and adjustments will be required of you in order for you to be disciplined in your walk toward the Inner Court.

2. What would you be willing to do for 30 days in order to intentionally walk into the Inner Court?

3. Ask someone to hold you accountable to these adjustments and commitments, and then go to that person and honestly share how it is going.

Let me remind you of something. It is quite comfortable in the Outer Court. In that Court, you can wander around having no expectations; you can do all the things you love to do in the church; you can stay dependent on others for your spiritual feeding. Yes, it is quite comfortable because so little is required of you. You can be lazy there and grow fat, but not on the food that will sustain you forever. The choice will always be yours. God has shown you that the Inner Court is right in front of you. But He will never drag you there. He might allow circumstances in your life to leave you feeling empty, but ultimately you must purpose to "go to school." Oswald Chambers put it this way:

> Many of us prefer to stay at the threshold of the Christian life instead of going on to construct a soul in accordance with the new life God has put within. We fail because we are ignorant of the way we are made; we put things down to the devil instead of our own undisciplined natures. Think what we can be when we are roused![6]

Do you prefer to stay at the threshold, barely in the door of the Tabernacle, because this undisciplined lifestyle requires nothing of you? Or do you desire to see your heart reconstructed and transformed into a heart that is undivided by satan, the world, and your own sin nature? Choosing to march straight for the Inner Court of your heart is the best decision you could make today! Are you ready? Go on now! Get out of your comfortable chair and start walking toward the Inner Court!

INTROSPECTION

1. As you look at the Tabernacle, what two initial experiences are common to the believer based on the symbolism of the bronze altar and laver?

2. What causes believers to stay longer in the Outer Court than they should?

3. How does resting in our belief in the sacrifice of Jesus and our baptism into His family stunt our spiritual growth?

4. Based on the layout of the Tabernacle, what is God's plan for our journey? Where do we begin? Where are we to end? Are we designed to stay in the Outer Court, the place of the beginning of our faith?

5. What personal and spiritual adjustments would you have to make in order to intentionally walk toward the Holy of Holies?

ENDNOTES

1. www.htmlbible.com/sacrednamebiblecom/kjvstrongs/CONHEB558. htm#S5582.

2. www.htmlbible.com/sacrednamebiblecom/kjvstrongs/CONHEB381. htm#S3820.

3. Spiros Zodhiates, *The Complete Word Study Dictionary: New Testament* (Chattanooga, TN: AMG Publishers, 1994), 99, #142, IV.

4. Zodhiates, *The Complete Word Dictionary: New Testament*, 792, #2508.

5. Bruce Wilkinson, *The Secrets of the Vine: Breaking Through to Abundance* (Sisters, OR: Multnomah Publishers, 2001), 34-35.

6. Oswald Chambers, *My Utmost for His Highest* (Grand Rapids, MI: Discovery House Publishers, 1963), 141.

CHAPTER 3

THE INNER COURT—
THE CLASSROOM

And do not be conformed to this world, but be transformed by the renewing of your mind, so that you may prove what the will of God is, that which is good and acceptable and perfect (Romans 12:2).

"A gray-haired old lady, long a member of her community and church, shook hands with the minister after the service one Sunday morning. 'That was a wonderful sermon,' she told him, 'just wonderful. Everything you said applies to someone I know.'"[1] Funny, but too true! That is the way that most people "hear" sermons or teachings. It seems to be for everyone but themselves. The next court that we will be peeking into is the Inner Court, the classroom for every believer. It is this court where we must leave the simple principles of faith behind and get serious about personally knowing the Teacher, the Holy Spirit, and learning from Him about the Word and worship.

MORE DESCRIPTIONS OF
THE COURTS OF THE TABERNACLE

Before we begin an in-depth look at the Inner Court of the Tabernacle, review again the chart of words that describe what takes place in each court.

THE OUTER COURT	THE INNER COURT	THE HOLY OF HOLIES
Introduction	Illumination	Intimacy
Discipline or Decision (Door)	Desire	Delight
Contrite Heart (Repentance of the totality of our sin)	Change of Heart	Complete Heart
The Way	The Truth	The Life
No fruit or little fruit	More fruit	Much fruit

Look again at the diagram of the Tabernacle. Are you seeing how they fit into their appropriate court based on the furnishings found in each?

Now let's add three more sets of words to the chart that will continue to help us clarify what happens in our hearts in each of the three courts.

THE OUTER COURT	THE INNER COURT	THE HOLY OF HOLIES
Justification	Sanctification	Glorification
Belief	Adjustment (Repentance of our individual daily sin)	Full Obedience
Jesus	Holy Spirit	Father

I learned the first set of words (justification, sanctification, and glorification) from a Kay Arthur study on the Book of First Peter. She called it "The Three Tenses of Salvation."[2] It also applies to the Tabernacle, as you will see. The justification of every believer takes place when we are declared "not guilty" by God because of our union with the crucified and risen Savior. It is an event that occurs the moment a new believer walks through the door of salvation in Christ. The sanctification process of every believer takes place at every point between the door and the Holy of Holies, but to a deeper and more focused way in the Inner Court. To be sanctified means to be set apart to God—from satan, from the world, and from our sin and flesh—for the sake of holiness and maturity. It is the transforming process of our walk. Our glorification takes place when we are standing in the very presence of God in Heaven, with a new glorified body. This is when God will honor His children.

In the second set of words (belief, adjustment, and full obedience), we can see that there are two different types of repentance that take place in the walk of a believer. The first is the repentance of a contrite heart that knows it is lost and will be forever separated from the love of Christ if He does not become your Savior. That repentance is for being a sinner, of Adam's race. But in the Inner Court, a different kind of repentance begins to take shape and become a common occurrence. It is the repentance of the individual sins that are the fruit of satan's influence, the world's influence, and the influence of our own sinful flesh. It is a repentance that recognizes and acknowledges daily sin, and it usually leads to the kind of walk that keeps very short accounts with God.

In the third set of words, we see that the Trinity of God also fits into the picture of the Tabernacle. Jesus made the way for us to enter into relationship with God through His ultimate sacrifice on the altar of the cross. When we receive Him as our personal Savior and we are baptized, it is into Jesus' family that we are adopted. We see Jesus in the Outer Court. The Inner Court is about the work of the Spirit within us that changes us from babies into mature Christians. When we receive our glorified bodies in Heaven, we will cast our crowns at the feet of Jesus in the presence of our Heavenly Father.

Refer back to this chart often so that you might keep clear in your mind the different parts of our journey that are represented in the three courts of the Tabernacle of our hearts.

A Closer Look at the Inner Court

Unlike the Outer Court of the Tabernacle, the Inner Court was only for the particular priests who would perform the services of the Tabernacle, services other than the sacrifices of the Outer Court. The people were not allowed to enter the Inner Court. It is noteworthy that the priests who entered the Inner Court were required to wash their feet and hands in the bronze laver before entering the Inner Court. It is conceivable that the hands needed to be washed in order to serve God in purity, and the feet needed to be washed in order to stand in purity while worshiping Him. But it was not a place of worship for those who were not priests to God.

Since we are talking about the Tabernacle of our hearts, we must understand that Jesus' death opened up a new way for all who would believe. As you look again at the model of the Tabernacle, can you clearly see what takes place in our hearts in the Inner Court? It is there that our sins will be more completely revealed to us by the illumination of the Spirit. It is in the Inner Court that we begin to have a desire for our sinful hearts to change as we read the Word and listen to the voice of the Spirit. It is in the Inner Court that we begin to bear the fruit of repentance—real heart and life change. It is in the warm glow of the Inner Court that we will begin to adjust how we think, talk, and live. And the Spirit is the One who will guide and teach us. As Christians, we must eventually go into the Inner Court, for *"who can say 'I have cleansed my heart, I am pure from my sin'?"* (Prov. 20:9). It is there that our hearts and our hands of service will be purified before the Lord.

THE COURT OF ALIGNMENT

Take a step back into the Outer Court. What takes place there? It is in the Outer Court that we repent of all of our sin in order to receive our salvation. Then the Spirit comes and dwells within us the moment we confess our sins and recognize that Jesus is the only way to Heaven. If we have been instructed correctly, we are then urged to be baptized in obedience to the Word of God, whereby we associate with and join ourselves to the Body of Christ by our identification with His death, burial, and resurrection.

Now, walk back into the Inner Court. Do you see that in the Inner Court the Spirit begins to work on our individual sins? Do you see the relevance of the lamp stand? The Spirit will also bring illumination to us through the Word, others, and our prayers to Him. And there the Spirit will also teach us what it means to truly worship God. In the Inner Court the Spirit and the Word act as our "spiritual chiropractors." God's will for us in the Inner Court is to see us adjusted and aligned with His Word and His will until we are consistently lined up with Him!

A few years ago, I was having some problems with my neck popping and cracking. I experienced headaches, neck aches, and back aches as a result. After putting up with this for several weeks, I finally decided to make an appointment with a chiropractor. After X-rays and an examination, I was set up for an on-going weekly treatment of chiropractic, heat therapy, and massage. The doctor had only one goal for me: to get me properly aligned in the core of my body so that the rest of my body could work appropriately. My spine needed to be adjusted so that it would be correctly aligned as it was created to be, not in the way that my life had realigned it. Do you see the correlation?

God can realign our spiritual lives when we enter the Inner Court. He can show us the way to line up with His will when we begin to read and study the Word. Lazily reading what we want in our Bibles, whenever we want, can never move us into full alignment with the will and purpose of God. Rare or sporadic time spent with God may have sufficed in the Outer Court, but it will not serve us well in the Inner Court of study. God cannot bring about our transformation and maturity until we stop refusing to spend concentrated time with Him. In the Inner Court, we will be striving after the daily part of "our daily bread." It is the place where we will learn to devour the bread, knowing that it is what sustains us. (See Psalm 104:15.)

God can realign our spiritual lives as well when we begin to listen to the Spirit as we study, pray, and go about our daily lives. As we listen, it will become more and more apparent to us that we must obey what we have heard, not just receive it as our next great new revelation or truth to ponder.

THE NECESSITY TO MOVE

When we are studying the Word, getting to know the voice of the Spirit, and obeying them both, we will begin to understand the meaning of the altar of incense, a place of worship in our journey. God calls us to worship Him in Spirit and in Truth. The Inner Court is just the place to learn how to worship that way. In the Inner Court, we will find ourselves moving from the elementary (beginning) teachings of the Outer Court to the deeper truths and practices of those who really want to follow Jesus into the Holy of Holies. Oswald Chambers saw it this way:

> If you do not cut the moorings, God will have to break them by a storm and send you out. Launch all on God, go out on the great swelling tide of His purpose, and you will get your eyes opened. If you believe in Jesus, you are not to spend all your time in the smooth waters just inside the harbor bar, full of delight, but always moored; you have to get out through the harbor bar into the great deeps of God and begin to know for yourself, begin to have spiritual discernment.[3]

Let's take a look at some verses from Hebrews that also support this thought. They will more clearly reveal our need to move from one court to the next.

> *For everyone who partakes only of milk is not accustomed to the word of righteousness, for he is an infant. But solid food is for the mature, who because of practice have their senses trained to discern good and evil Therefore leaving the elementary teaching about the Christ, let us press on to maturity, not laying again a foundation of repentance from dead works and of faith toward God* (Hebrews 5:13–14; 6:1).

Do you see in these verses a progression through the Tabernacle? The milk provides our nourishment in the Outer Court. As new believers, we all had to learn the basic foundational principles concerning our new faith. Walking in the Spirit, obedience to the Word, and uninhibited worship were concepts that we didn't understand in the Outer Court of our salvation. But this is the solid food that awaits our hungry hearts in the Inner Court of the Tabernacle. As we eat of this solid food of the Inner Court, we begin to understand more clearly the need for a heart change so that we can live righteously. This food was not intended for babes in the Lord, but it was most definitely intended for those who desire to grow and mature into true disciples of Christ. Having laid our firm foundation of faith in Him by our repentance, we have walked in the Outer Court of these elementary principles. But we must, at some point in our journey, press on to the maturity that is born out of the Inner Court experience. Read again the Hebrews verses. Do they make sense to you now?

Jesus quoted the prophet Isaiah when He said in Matthew 15:8, *"This people honors Me with their lips, but their heart is far away from Me."* As we step into the Inner Court, we begin to study the Word of God, to hear and know the Spirit's voice, to obey Him, and to truly worship God with our whole heart and life. Then our heart is no longer far away from Him. We find intimacy in His nearness and realize that the Holy of Holies is far closer to us than it was when we were wandering around in the Outer Court. This is a wonderful picture of "drawing near to God."

THE COURT OF HEART TRANSFORMATION

In the Inner Court, our walk with Jesus will be all about what is going on inside of our hearts. We claim our Christianity with our mouths in the Outer Court, but often we remain very distant from the God who saved us. However, in the Inner Court, God begins to align the things we say and believe with how we act. For Him to do that, He has to begin to weed out the sin that remained in our hearts and minds after our salvation, those individual sins that keep us in a sin-confess-sin-confess cycle. His weeding process occurs through the Spirit's conviction and the Word's truth spoken directly to our hearts. They begin to affect everything about us! No longer are we satisfied with merely saying we are Christians. Our heart's desire is to become Christlike. We begin to want to live out our Christianity by learning the Word and doing what it demands of us. It is in the Inner Court that we begin to obey out of a heart that is changing, a heart that is more aligned, one that desires to bring glory to God through obedience.

THE COURT OF DEATH

In the Inner Court, we will be bringing our whole hearts to God, bit by sinful bit. It will be hard work for us as we begin to sacrifice our selfish desires and pleasures and learn to walk in obedience instead of following our flesh. In the Inner Court, we will understand with all certainty that our flesh must die!

Observe how this verse from John 12:24 also lines up with the process of our hearts in the Inner Court that I have just described:

> *Truly, truly, I say to you, unless a grain of wheat falls into the earth and dies, it remains alone; but if it dies, it bears much fruit.*

The crucifixion of our flesh at the veil in the Inner Court leads to bearing much spiritual fruit. And we have already determined that "much fruit" is borne out of us when we are walking in the Holy of Holies. It should be clear to you now that the Inner Court is the place where the Lord works on the heart issues that keep us from the intimacy of the presence of God on an ongoing basis.

Let's compare now the deaths that occur in both courts and what was overcome by those deaths. In the Outer Court, Jesus was the One who died. That is made clear in the symbolism of the bronze altar. His death overcame our sentence of death. But when we were saved, we did not stop sinning completely because our flesh was, and still is, sinful. So His death did not remove sin from us. His death removed from us the power of sin and death over us. The penalty was removed, but our sinful, wicked flesh remained.

Now let's look at the death that takes place in the Inner Court. Who dies there? We do! Our flesh does! When our hearts are educated in the Inner Court classroom, we begin to walk in the Spirit instead of our flesh because we are daily crucifying it. As a part of the process, we start walking in the Light of God's Word as well, instead of continuing in the darkness of our daily sins. In the Inner Court, we also learn to fellowship with God through a worship-filled life. Jesus' flesh is the veil, and at the moment He died on the cross, the veil was rent in two from top to bottom. He opened up for us a way to personally relate intimately with our Holy Father, being able to come boldly to His throne. In the same manner, the crucifying of our flesh, our truest worship, is our entrance into the Holy of Holies. John 4:23 confirms this:

But an hour is coming, and now is, when the true worshipers will worship the
Father in spirit and truth...

We can now put our Tabernacle divisions of Jesus-Spirit-Father all
together. Jesus is the Door and the sacrifice on the bronze altar of the
Outer Court, and our baptism identifies us with Him. In the Inner Court,
we learn to be true worshipers of God by beginning to worship in Spirit
and in the truth of the Word. And who are we addressing and aiming that
worship toward? We aim our worship toward the Father who resides in
the Holy of Holies.

It would be fruitless for us to try to enter the Holy of Holies any
other way. We must come through the door and through the veil. It is
only when we are standing before the altar of incense (worship) with
crucified flesh that the veil of our hearts is torn away, opening a way for
us into the very presence of God. If we are looking in any other direction but toward the Holy of Holies and the face of God, then we will
not be facing the One we are seeking. We cannot enter into His presence
walking backward! If we are "dying" in the Inner Court, we are heading
in the right direction—straight into the Holy of Holies.

There is a spiritual picture for us to see in the last plague on the
Egyptians during the days of Moses that can be applied to the dying of
our flesh. The last plague of God upon Pharaoh and all of Egypt was the
plague of death. In order for the Israelites to survive this plague, they were
required to sacrifice a lamb and put its blood on the frames of the doors
of their homes. They were told by God to do this so that the angel of
death would "pass over" them. They were also told to eat a specific meal
that particular night that included unleavened bread. One reason it was to
be unleavened (without yeast) was so they would be ready to make their
exodus very quickly.

But I offer to you another theory. I believe we are being given another picture of our journey through the Tabernacle. We know that
Jesus was our sacrificial Lamb, and that His shed blood, when applied
to our lives through salvation, saves us from death. This is the picture of
the Outer Court. As we move from the Outer Court to the Inner Court,

we are to be in the process of turning from our sin. Did you know that in the New Testament sinfulness is often referred to as leaven? We are told in Luke 12:1 to *"beware of the leaven of the Pharisees."* Jesus was referring to their lifestyle of sinful pride. In the very next verse He says, *"But there is nothing covered up that will not be revealed, and hidden that will not be known."* In the Inner Court, we are to become like unleavened bread, without sin. In the Inner Court, our sins will be illuminated by the Spirit and the Word so that they can be dealt with. In the Inner Court, we can no longer cover up our sins or let them remain hidden in the folds of our sinful hearts.

Do you get the picture? Jesus did His part of preparing a way for a deep and intimate relationship with us and a way to take us to the Father. After we have received Him and have been baptized into Him, we must do our part. We must obey the call on our lives to be purified and perfected because we are called to a walk in the Spirit in holiness.

PAUL'S EXAMPLE

But how can we make our rotten flesh holy? We can't, for it is forever tainted with the sin of Adam. But we can put it to death so that the holiness of the Spirit within us can rule our lives. Paul understood this principle, for he said, *"I die daily"* (I Cor. 15:31). By that he meant that he surrendered his will to God daily; he sought to put to death his flesh daily through that surrender; he began a walk of putting God's priorities and desires ahead of his own; and he sacrificed the life he would normally be living on his own, without God, for a life marked by obedience to everything God instructed him to do. So in essence, Paul adjusted himself to God's way. He allowed the Spirit to be his personal and spiritual chiropractor, the One who adjusted him on a daily basis by the truth. In that way, Paul died daily and was constantly being aligned with the purposes of God. Paul certainly knew what it was like to be a student in the classroom of the Inner Court and a patient on God's "chiropractic table."

So now, here's the question. If you are currently in the Inner Court, are you being adjusted by Dr. Holy Spirit? Is He your chiropractor? Are you receiving His daily treatments? If not, you might have the same problem I once had—availability to Him. To be adjusted by the Holy Spirit, you must make yourself available to Him. If I want my chiropractor to give me a treatment, I have to make an appointment and then keep it!

While the Outer Court can be likened to a school playground, the Inner Court is, without doubt, your spiritual classroom. It is the place where you will be learning to live in a deep and abiding relationship with God. Do you remember from the first chapter that this is what God desires of us? Are you also beginning to understand that God desires greatly for your heart to be healed and transformed? He wants desperately for you to experience spiritual healing. He seeks to make you holy!

THE HIGHWAY TO HOLINESS

In *Having a Mary Heart in a Martha World*, Joanna Weaver compares Mary's and Martha's responses to Jesus coming to their home. Martha, the consummate hostess, busied herself with all the preparations for the evening meal. She became irritated and frustrated with her sister, who just sat on the floor listening to the Master. Martha was in the kitchen (the Outer Court) of busy-ness and to-do lists, and her emotions were prone to take over. She was all about her external appearance. Mary, on the other hand, knew what the "better part" was. It was to allow her hungry heart to be fed. So she sat in the living room of intimacy with her Lord and Savior, basking in His words of faith and wisdom, unashamedly sitting with the men while her sister labored in the kitchen. The author implies that while Martha's way may have been safer, it certainly was not better!

> "Intimacy can be threatening. Getting close to Jesus means we can no longer hide our inadequacies. His light illuminates everything that is wrong and ugly about our lives. Unconsciously, therefore, we may flee God's presence rather than pursue it. And Satan spurs on our retreat by telling us we're not good enough to earn God's favor. He tells us that when we get our act together—that's when we can enter the Living Room. But

the truth is, we can't get our spiritual act together unless we go to the Living Room first.[4]

We are on a spiritual path. We have walked through the Door, received our salvation, and been baptized. The next step on the journey is the straight and narrow "highway of holiness," the journey to living out God's commandments in full.

If you read Isaiah 35:8-10, you will discover that it is our choice to be wise or foolish (8). You can't walk on the Highway of Holiness and remain in your sin. When we walk in holiness though, the road, the Way (Jesus) will be there for us. On this pathway, we will not be devoured by the enemy anymore (9). Satan will have less and less power over us because our flesh will be dying more and more. And on this highway, we will return to God and His ways through our repentance of going our way. We will be found turning away from our goals, attitudes, and sins and toward His. This roadway will lead us into an everlasting joy and gladness where our sorrow and sighing are gone (10)! And what does that sound like? It sounds like the Holy of Holies to me! Standing in the very real presence of God! Now we can understand Romans 12:1-2 with greater clarity:

> Therefore I urge you, brethren, by the mercies of God, to present your bodies a living and holy sacrifice, acceptable to God, which is your spiritual service of worship. (12:1)

The presenting of our bodies is the crucifying of our flesh, even as it was for Jesus when He went to the cross. He presented His body to be crucified. When we do this, it is a gift of holy service and worship to God. He readily accepts this kind of sacrifice from us. Dying to our flesh is the worship He responds to and desires for us. Dying is what we are to do on the Inner Court side of the veil at the altar of incense.

> And do not be conformed to this world, but be transformed by the renewing of your mind, so that you may prove what the will of God is, that which is good and acceptable and perfect. (12:2)

In the Inner Court of alignment, our minds become transformed by the Spirit and the Word. Our worldly and fleshly ways morph into goodness, holy behavior, and our being perfected (made mature and complete). The Word says in Philippians 1:6, *"He who began a good work in you will perfect [complete] it until the day of Christ Jesus."* This perfecting and maturing has not yet been completed in us, but from the time we walked through the Door, God has been at work in us while we were in the Outer Court and certainly while dwelling in the Inner Court. The heart is made ready to the greatest degree in the Inner Court. It is there that our hearts are fashioned for His presence.

This is what it is like to be standing in the Inner Court. You are bringing your whole heart and life to God. Your eyes are firmly fixed on the God beyond the veil. You are consistently breaking through the sins of your heart. You are intentionally setting out to walk through the entire Tabernacle. You have not taken the easy way, but have arisen from your comfortable chair of complacency. Your goal is out in front of you; completeness, perfection, and Christian maturity come from dying to your flesh, your very own Calvary. Entering into the Holy of Holies has become your heart song, your life's goal.

THE PARABLE OF THE HILL

Let me share with you the song of my own heart. This song of my journey came in the form of a parable from God's heart to mine one day when I was walking the hills of my neighborhood and praying. May it bless you, as it did me.

One day a girl looked over her life and realized that she was blessed to have life and breath. They were gifts to her, but they couldn't be all that life was supposed to be. Lately, she had put on several unwanted pounds, and she was not happy about that at all! They had slipped on, unnoticed for awhile, because of wrong choices made: wrong food, too little exercise, and laziness. She knew that if she didn't do something, they could prove fatal. You see, she had a very bad genealogy when it came to hearts: her paternal grandfather and uncle, and even her own father, had died of massive heart attacks. Surely she was to pay attention to this matter of the heart.

With discipline and determination, she set out to walk off those extra pounds. The first day she slowly walked a three-mile route by her home. It was hilly and hard work. It was not the most fun thing she had ever done, but she did it, and afterward she felt quite good about it. But one good day of walking would not take care of her heart problem. So the next day she walked the path again. Going up and down all those hills winded her. But again she finished the task and felt the better for it. Day after day for a couple of weeks, she walked and huffed and puffed and smiled at the end (but only at the end!).

After several days of walking, she realized something very important. If she was going to get the maximum benefit of walking, she would have to push harder, walk faster, and burn more calories. It could no longer be a leisurely stroll. It must become a workout! It needed to be the kind of workout that would strengthen her heart. The days of the comfortable walk were over!

With a new resolve, she set out to push herself. But in so doing, she discovered that walking the hills at a faster pace caused her to struggle. Sometimes she just wanted to quit and go back to the days of the stroll. Every hill seemed like Mount Everest to her. Her muscles burned, her heart raced, and her breath came very short. Oh, how she wanted to slow down. No! She wanted to stop and go home to her comfy chair! But instead, she pressed on.

As the days turned into weeks, and the weeks into months, she realized that she was getting stronger and stronger. Her discipline to walk her way to better health had become a desire to her, and the exercise was paying off. Pushing herself to be healthier and stronger was bringing the desired results. Muscles were firming, excess weight and inches were vanishing, and people were noticing the changes. But one truth remained: no matter how strong she became, there would always be another hill to climb. Giving up was no longer an option. Hill climbing would need to be a part of her life for the rest of her life! And the only way to make it to the top of a hill was to keep her eye on the ultimate goal. And of course, to never stop climbing!

We have sin in our hearts to overcome. They are the "hills" we must scale on the path to the Holy of Holies. The journey of gaining victory over those hills will not be an easy one. It may even (and likely will!) get harder as God roots out of us our most difficult sins. But the benefits will be great, and others will notice the changes. Then we will be able to have a wonderful testimony to them that will bring glory to God. But what is the key to attaining to that kind of life? Keeping your eyes on the goal and continuing to climb over the hills! We will learn how to practically apply these principles in the chapters ahead. Will you continue with me on this journey to an unbroken heart? I can't make you. And the Spirit will not drag you along. The choice is yours. It's up to you. Are you ready to make that journey?

Why not pray about it right now and then respond to God's sweet voice? He is calling you, if you are roaming around in the Outer Court, to draw nearer to Him by walking toward the Inner Court classroom. Can you make a commitment to God to do what it takes to get there? And if you are already abiding in the Inner Court, can you prayerfully ask God to reveal to you the work of the next "grade level" of His classroom? Or maybe it is time for Him to reveal another sin to you that He wants you to overcome. Can you commit to doing whatever it takes to crucify all of your flesh? Remember—God's desire for you is to walk intimately with Him. But He won't move your feet (and heart) for you.

Go ahead. Jump into the deeper waters that will flood your soul with joy and bring a smile to your Father's face! Read on. There will be more on how to crucify your flesh in the chapters ahead. For now, begin to dig into the Word and learn from the Spirit. Eat your daily bread, and let the Spirit illuminate the truth to you. Go on now. Get started!

INTROSPECTION

I. The Inner Court is like an intense classroom. How willing are you to be taught by the Holy Spirit and His illumination of the Word?

2. God is looking for people who will honor Him with their whole hearts. What does He see when He looks into your heart? Does it line up with what He hears you say or sees you do?

3. What sins in your heart need to be aligned with the Word of God and His good will for you?

4. The Inner Court experience ends at the veil. Are you prepared to undergo the process of dying daily?

5. Do you truly desire a greater level of intimacy with God?

ENDNOTES

1. *Bits & Pieces* (November, 1989), 19, www.sermonillustrations.com/a-z/a/application.htm.

2. Kay Arthur, *I Peter: In and Out* (Chattanooga, TN: Precept Ministries International, 2003), 13.

3. Oswald Chambers, *My Utmost for His Highest* (Grand Rapids, MI: Discovery House Publishers, 1963), 160.

4. Joanna Weaver, *Having a Mary Heart in a Martha World* (Colorado Springs, CO: Waterbrook Press, 2002), 60.

CHAPTER 4

THE HOLY OF HOLIES—
LIVING IN THE
PRESENCE OF GOD

Therefore, brethren, since we have confidence to enter the holy place [the Holy of Holies] *by the blood of Jesus. . .let us draw near* (Hebrews 10:19,22a).

There are Christians who, in seeking salvation, only think of themselves and their own happiness: Christ is simply a means to an end. There are others who go farther: they feel a personal relation to Christ, and desire greatly to know and serve Him better. But even with these, there is something lacking which is indispensable to a whole and vigorous Christian character. They do not know that Christ is only the way, the door to the Father, and that His great desire is to lead us through and past Himself to the Father, really to bring us to God![1]

Do you see the amazing likeness Andrew Murray's words have to the Tabernacle we have been studying? He has shown us three types of Christians: an Outer Court Christian, and Inner Court Christian, and a Holy of Holies Christian! The truth of his words reveal a secret that will help us understand our need to move through the Tabernacle and reach our goal of living within the Holy of Holies. "God is not content that we should serve Him with a veil between. Let us know clearly which of the two positions we occupy as Christians—within or still without the veil."[2] It is critical that we know where we stand in the Tabernacle! "Fifteen hundred years the veil had to hang with it solemn injunction not to draw near...."[3] The veil has been rent by Christ's death and our death to our flesh. It is time to draw near to the Father!

But before we continue with our study of the Tabernacle by looking at the Holy of Holies, we would be wise to pause a moment and reflect on what we have already learned. How are you doing with this journey through the heart of your walk with God? Maybe a better question would be what are you doing with what you have learned? Did the end of the previous chapter motivate you to take a determined next step out of your comfort zone?

Maybe some heart-piercing questions still remain. Are you seeing any evidence of the fruit of spiritual growth that comes with drawing closer to God? Are you experiencing the closeness of God throughout the day or more than you have previously? Did God reveal to your heart and mind any individual sins for which you are to repent? Have you seen the truths of the Tabernacle changing your heart? If you have, take a moment to thank the Holy Spirit for showing and teaching you what you needed to know right now. If you can't see how this is helping you draw nearer to God, do not despair! More practical application is on the way in the following chapters! Continue to focus on seeing your heart united and unbroken so you can fear God's name. Be determined to see it changed for His glory! Press on to further understand the Old Testament's picture of the walk of a New Testament Christian!

WHAT WE GAIN

Does your heart have room for more divisional word sets? We will look at one now and some others later in this chapter. Let's look at how we have previously defined the courts.

THE OUTER COURT	THE INNER COURT	THE HOLY OF HOLIES
Introduction	Illumination	Intimacy
Discipline or Decision (Door)	Desire	Delight
Contrite Heart (Repentance of the totality of our sin)	Change of Heart	Complete Heart
The Way	The Truth	The Life
No fruit or little fruit	More fruit	Much fruit

THE OUTER COURT	THE INNER COURT	THE HOLY OF HOLIES
Justification	Sanctification	Glorification
Belief	Adjustment (Repentance of our individual daily sin)	Full Obedience
Jesus	Holy Spirit	Father

Now, here is yet another way to view the Tabernacle courts:

Gain the Name (Christian)	Gain the Relationship	Gain God's Continual Presence

When we step through the Door of belief with a contrite and repentant heart for our sin nature, knowing that Jesus is not only our way to God but also that which gives us the ability to be cleansed from the totality of all of our sin (justification in God's book), we gain the name of our Savior, Jesus Christ. In our identification with Him and all that He did for us on the cross, we became His children by adoption into the family of God. At the very instant that we believed, we gained His name—Christian. What a glorious gift is given to any child adopted into a family. Receiving the name of our Savior gives us a strong foundation for who we are to become. We are to be like Jesus. We are to grow up into Christlikeness. And it all begins with a prayer of belief in Him and being given His name.

As we have seen in great detail in the previous chapter, the Inner Court is all about gaining a more personal relationship with God through the Spirit's influence in our lives. He uses the Word of God to illuminate the individual sins in our life so that we can see our definite need for realigning with what the Word tells us. The Holy Spirit causes us to grow in our desire to spend time with Him. In the Inner Court, the Holy Spirit seems to be more committed to taking us down the Highway of Holiness, which is our sanctification process. It is the place where we learn to walk out a daily, holy lifestyle, knowing that God has given us a definite call to "be holy because He is holy." The Inner Court is all about this relationship for sure.

As we progress in the areas of walking in the Spirit and in holiness, we are led out of the Inner Court and into the Holy of Holies when our flesh begins to die. When everything God desires of us supersedes everything our flesh desires for us, we are getting extremely close to the sheer delight of the intimacy that can be found in the Father's manifest presence in our lives. In the Holy of Holies, we find that our hearts have matured to the point that Jesus is everything to us, and that our obedience to His will has filled our basket of "fruit" to overflowing. Ultimately we will step through the veil of our own dead flesh one final time. Then we will know the rapture of being in His eternal presence and living in glorified bodies made to worship Him forever. Our journey through the Tabernacle of a heart relationship to God is what will find us dwelling with Him forever!

SALVATION'S PROGRESSIVE NATURE

Oswald Chambers agrees that our salvation is not what happens when we ask Jesus into our hearts. It is a process that only begins there. See if you can see our progression through the Tabernacle in what he says.

Salvation is not merely deliverance from sin, nor the experience of personal holiness; the salvation of God is deliverance out of self entirely into union with Himself.[4]

"Deliverance from sin" is our Outer Court experience. "Personal holiness" is our Inner Court experience. Complete deliverance from self into union with God is what the Holy of Holies experience is all about. Maybe Colossians 3:3-5 best describes this:

> *For you have died and your life is hidden with Christ in God. When Christ, who is our life, is revealed, then you also will be revealed with Him in glory. Therefore, consider the members of your earthly body as dead to immorality, impurity, passion, evil desire, and greed, which amounts to idolatry.*

This is the picture I have of the Holy of Holies experience: that I have died (my flesh is crucified, which tears the veil), the life that was once mine and all about me is now dead, wrapped up in Christ, and He now lives His life through me.

I personally understand least the Court of the Holy of Holies. I cannot speak much from my own journey…yet! My salvation is progressive, and I am still in process! The Court of the Holy of Holies is what I am currently straining toward, but I still have so much to learn in the Inner Court. So much more of my heart is in need of transformation. But even with my inadequate experience, the Word has much to say about this often elusive place. It can and will teach us what we need to know for the journey there. The Books of Isaiah and Romans will help us understand the court of God's presence, the court of intimacy.

GLADNESS OF HEART

The ninth chapter of Isaiah has some very familiar verses that are used quite often at Christmas, the season of Advent. Verse 6 has probably been made most famous by Handel's use of it in the renowned work "The Messiah." The strains of "for unto us a Child is born, unto us a Son is given" ring true in our hearts as we celebrate the birth of Christ. Because he included them in his masterpiece, parts of these

Scriptures have reached to the ends of the earth. But I want us to look at these now in a different light. We will soon see how Handel himself must have personally understood the Christian journey.

We will start with three verses that precede the more familiar ones. Isaiah 9:2-4 reads like this:

> *The people who walk in darkness will see a great light; those who live in a dark land, the light will shine on them. You shall multiply the nation, you shall increase their gladness; they will be glad in Your presence as with the gladness of harvest, as men rejoice when they divide the spoil. For You shall break the yoke of their burden and the staff on their shoulders, the rod of their oppressor, as at the battle of Midian.*

"The people who walk in darkness will see a great light.... What does that remind you of? Did you think of the star of Bethlehem? Or maybe you thought of the day when Jesus, the Light of the World, came to you. Do you recall the darkness that you were living in before you were saved? Where in the Tabernacle did the Light first shine on your darkness? It was in the Outer Court where the Light of Jesus began to illuminate your path. Light began to shine on and through you at the point of your salvation. Looking further at these three verses, we see that the presence of God is mentioned, as well as its effect on us. When we are in His presence, our gladness is increased and will be experienced every time we are with Him.

Investigating further in verse 3, we can get a clearer view of the court where God dwells. Before we delve into that, though, let's let the Hebrew dictionary define for us the word "glad". The literal meaning is from a primitive root word meaning "to make joyful or cause to rejoice, to brighten up, making the heart merry, being gleeful."[5] Gladness of heart should translate to the face. When we are glad, our faces show it, and others know it! What kind of fruit do you think we would bear if the lost actually saw the light of Jesus in the gladness of our bright and joyful countenances?

Now, where does this verse say that we will *be glad*? It says that we will be glad in God's presence, and we have already learned that His dwelling is in the Holy of Holies. But before we go on, let me clarify something. I am not saying that God does not reside in any other court. Quite the opposite is true. We see God the Son in the Door and as the sacrifice on the altar of the Outer Court. We see God the Spirit in the light of the lamp stands that illuminate our way. Also we see God the Spirit in the true worship that is produced in Spirit and in truth in the Inner Court. But God the Father's "dwelling" presence is in the Holy of Holies between the wings of the cherubim on the mercy seat of the Ark of the Covenant. And that is where we are glad!

Isaiah even tells us to what degree we will be glad. We will experience gladness in His presence in increased levels, just like in the days of harvest when the bounty of the land is brought in. Our gladness will be like a great harvest. Do you see the correlation between the great harvest and bearing much fruit? Isaiah also likens this increase of gladness to the joy of men who bring home the undeserved blessings of the spoil of war—the booty! Our word groups for the courts of the Tabernacle continue to line up with the biblical descriptions of each court! Isn't that amazing?

When Sin Is No Longer Master

Now, switching gears, we will look at what Isaiah shares about Jesus, who will be the one to *"break the yoke of* [our] *burden and the staff on* [our] *shoulders."* The yoke of our burden is identified in the first two verses of Romans 8:

> *Therefore there is now no condemnation for those who are in Christ Jesus.*
> *For the law of the Sprit of life in Christ Jesus has set you free from the law*
> *of sin and death.*

Our yoke is sin and death. We receive this gift of a broken yoke at the time of our salvation. It is realized in our daily walk more and more in the classroom of the Inner Court. But it is in the presence of Almighty God that we can lay claim to this verse:

For sin shall not be master over you, for you are not under law but under grace (Romans 6:14).

Look back now again at the drawing of the Tabernacle. Why did Jesus have to break the yoke of sin and death for us? He did it because they were an eternal burden to us that would have kept us from the Father forever. This burden was placed upon us by satan when Adam and Eve disobeyed God's command to not eat of the Tree of the knowledge of Good and Evil. When they sinned, all mankind came under the curse of sin and death. Without Jesus, no one could be saved because satan's curse and our sin nature would always prevent us from attaining eternal life. Jesus is the only One who could break the yoke of sin and death! Jesus is the only Way, the only Truth, and the only Life!

When Jesus took our sins upon Himself, was crucified on the cross of Calvary, died, and was resurrected, He became the Door into a relationship with God. It is through this relationship with Him that we are justified, sanctified, and glorified. Can you see how these three words can easily define what happens in each of the three courts as well?

When we enter the Tabernacle by faith in Jesus, we are no longer under the curse of sin and death. In the Outer Court, we begin a walk of justification that we gained by our belief in Christ, the Son of God, who can take away the condemnation of our sin nature. In the Inner Court— interestingly enough, also called the Holy Place—we begin to root out the specific sins of our lives. It is there that we begin a walk of holiness (or sanctification), learning to be holy because our holy God calls His children to be holy, as well. Then, as we walk through the veil of our crucified flesh, we catch glimpses of the presence of God our Father, actively at work in a very present sort of way. Eventually we will receive our glorified bodies when our physical bodies die. Do you remember Kay Arthur's "Three Tenses of Salvation"? Just like the courts of the Tabernacle, we enter these stages progressively.

A LOOK AT THE TRINITY

Skipping back now to Isaiah 9, let's continue with verse 6:

For a child will be born to us, a son will be given to us; and the government will rest on His shoulders; and His name will be called Wonderful Counselor, Mighty God, Eternal Father, Prince of Peace.

Do you remember adding the Trinity to our chart in the last chapter? In Isaiah 9, we once again can see the Trinity. These names are not merely names we recall at Christmas that sound wonderful together, especially in this song of Handel. They are a picture of God in His fullness! Do we not refer to the Holy Spirit as our Counselor? Eternal Father is self-explanatory. And the Prince of Peace is none other than Jesus Christ. This picture of our Mighty God—the Holy Trinity—is captured in just one little verse!

THE IMPORTANCE OF
OUR POWER OVER SIN AND DEATH

But we must take an even closer look at this verse to better understand how it points to the activity in the Holy of Holies. Looking at just one word in detail from verse 6 will help us to grasp where we have to be in our journey to holiness in order to find ourselves in the Holy of Holies here on earth. The word we need to investigate is "government." *"And the government will rest on His shoulders."*

Today, if you asked anyone who is old enough to vote what the meaning of the word "government" might be, you would probably receive answers something like these:

- "The men who make and uphold the laws of the land."
- "The rules that our nation lives by."
- "Those who have authority over us."
- "The people we must obey."
- "The seat of power of our nation."

In the original Hebrew, "government" means about the same as our English dictionaries would define it, with just a few nuances. The Hebrew would add these to its definition: empire; to have power; to prevail.

Jesus prevailed over sin and death, abolishing forever their influence on believers. Jesus spoke of this "prevailing" during a pivotal conversation that He had with Peter and the disciples. When Jesus asked them, *"Who do people say that the Son of Man is?"* their answers were varied, but not one of them was right. Some thought He was John the Baptist and others thought He might be Elijah. Still, others thought He could possibly be Jeremiah or one of the other prophets. Jesus questioned them on what their responses were to the multitudes who were speculating. *"But who do you say that I am?"* (Matt.16:15-16). *"Simon Peter answered, 'You are the Christ, the Son of the living God.'"*

Jesus was pleased with this answer and after blessing him for his response, Jesus said this to him:

> *I also say to you that you are Peter, and upon this rock I will build My church; and the gates of Hades will not overpower it* (Matthew 16:18).

Are you beginning to get the connection? Jesus prevailed, once and for all, over sin and death, and those who choose to believe in and follow Him will enjoy the fruit of that "prevailing." The Church would be built upon the rock, not Peter the rock, but the rock-solid foundation of this power over sin and death accomplished by Christ's sacrificial death on the cross. This foundation is to be built upon. We see its importance in the Outer Court where we learn to stand in the truth of Christ's sacrifice and victory over sin and death. It is the foundation of our faith. We also see it in the Inner Court as we begin to put to death our own daily sin. But it is in the Holy of Holies where this overpowering sees its greatest reward.

We are called to place the full government of our lives, the entirety of our hearts, onto the shoulders of Jesus. And the government of our lives is to rest there upon *His* shoulders. Do you remember the yoke that was on our shoulders, the yoke that Jesus broke when He prevailed over sin and death? Though the yoke was broken, we often find another yoke to step back into when we choose to continue in our sin, the yoke of bondage to the sin. This bondage to our daily sin is the very government Jesus was created to shoulder. But the only way He can do this is through our surrender, brokenness, and repentance. That is the only way that He can gain full authority over our hearts and lives; it is the only way that He will have full control over us. When He is our Ruler, then we will have proven by our surrender that He has prevailed in us!

CONTINUAL FRUIT AND PEACE

This picture shows what it looks like to dwell in the Holy of Holies. When our lives are resting comfortably on the shoulders of Jesus, then we can honestly say that we are allowing Jesus to have His rightful place of authority and rule over everything in our lives. It is when we make Him more than our Savior and more than our Lord and Master. We will know His daily presence when we make Him our everything! Our all, the Boss of me! He will then be the only authority of my life—my Ruler. He will be on the throne of my life then—not me.

This is the ultimate goal in our journey on this earth. And the fruitful blessing of reaching the Holy of Holies can be found in the very next verse:

There will be no end to the increase of His government or of peace (Isaiah 9:7a).

It is clear that the more we give Him the throne of our lives and allow Him to rule our hearts, actions, and thoughts, the more peace will increase in our hearts. There has never been a generation that seeks peace more than this one. Yet, a journey through the Tabernacle, all the way through, is the only way for us to realize this kind of peace—the peace that passes all understanding. Inner peace is the result of our surrender to God as the Savior of our lives, the Lord of our lives, and the Ruler of our lives. This is living in the presence of God!

> To be so much in contact with God that you never need to ask Him to show you His will, is to be nearing the final stage of your discipline in the life of faith. When you are rightly related to God, it is a life of freedom and liberty and delight.[6]

CONTEMPLATING THE COURTS

Now I am simply going to add six more words to our chart that continue to define the courts of the Tabernacle. Look for them at the bottom of the chart. Be watching for more that you can add to this chart as you continue to study the Bible and its principles. Take a moment now to review them. My prayer is that you will have a deeper understanding of the journey you are on by this in-depth study of the Tabernacle as a picture of your heart on this journey.

THE OUTER COURT	THE INNER COURT	THE HOLY OF HOLIES
Introduction	Illumination	Intimacy
Discipline or Decision (Door)	Desire	Delight
Contrite Heart (Repentance of the totality of our sin)	Change of Heart	Complete Heart
The Way	The Truth	The Life
No fruit or little fruit	More fruit	Much fruit
Justification	Sanctification	Glorification
Belief	Adjustment (Repentance of our individual daily sin)	Full Obedience
Jesus	Holy Spirit	Father
Gain the Name (Christian)	Gain the Relationship	Gain God's continual Presence
My Savior	My Lord/Master	My All/Ruler/King
Pardon	Purity	Paradise (rest)
Faith	Hope	Love (the greatest)

THE CHRIST OF THE TABERNACLE

This chart can be a helpful tool as you continue to gain a deeper understanding of the journey that you have undertaken. As we contemplate one final review of the entire Tabernacle, I again pray that it will become engraved on your minds. This is the walk of a Christian.

Travel with me now through the Tabernacle of your ever-growing and intensifying walk toward and within the Holy of Holies. Look again at the picture of the Tabernacle. Imagine (or draw in) a red line that connects the Door all the way to the Ark of the Covenant as we review. Using the words from our chart, I will describe this awesome journey. We enter the Tabernacle through our belief by faith in Jesus the Door. He is the Way in! Jesus becomes our Savior when we enter. We are saved and baptized, and we identify ourselves with Christ by taking His name (Christian). In this court of our introduction to a personal relationship with Christ, we bring to Him a contrite heart, confessing and repenting to Him our sin nature. We are justified in God's eyes regarding that sin nature, having gained our pardon. We begin to bear fruit for His Kingdom out of our newfound love for Him. By discipline we open the Word, discover basic truth, and learn to pray. These lead us to the door of the Inner Court. (Did you draw the red line from the Door to the Inner Court?)

Continue drawing that red line as you visualize stepping into the Inner Court. It is there that the light of the Spirit begins to illuminate our minds to understand and live out the truth of the Word. Our obedience to the Spirit and the Word begins to reveal in us a changed heart. As we begin to do all that He commands us to do, we see that our lives are being adjusted to God's will for us. This whole process of walking toward holiness and purity is called sanctification. Our relationship deepens, and our desire to spend time with God grows in intensity. We find that Jesus is more than just our Savior. He has become our Lord and Master. Because He is controlling so much more of our hearts, we become believers who bear even more fruit.

Are you still traveling through the Tabernacle with me? Keep drawing that red line as you pass through the veil, the place of the death of your flesh, and step into the Holy of Holies. Because of the crucifixion of our flesh, we have become more and more Christlike in all that we think, say, and do. Greater intimacy with God occurs as we begin to die daily. As this occurs, it becomes sheer delight to obey the Father. Our hearts are nearly complete (perfected and healed), and the abundance of fruit in our lives is a testimony that God is the only life we desire. He is our all in all, and He has complete rule of our hearts. It is in the Holy of Holies that we stand daily in the very presence of God, paradise on earth, putting our hope and trust in Him for the day we set foot in Heaven, paradise on high, where our bodies will finally be glorified.

So, as you can see, our journey as believers is to be constantly lining up with God! This is the Walk of Alignment that leads us home. But we haven't completed the lining up of the Tabernacle yet! Now for the coolest part!

Do you see that red line from the Door to the Ark of the Covenant? Now draw a new red line beginning at the lamp stand and running through the table of showbread. Do you see it? Our lines have created a red cross on the inside of the Tabernacle! This entire journey has been made possible for us by the blood that Christ shed for us on the cross of Calvary. This journey for us is what God purposed for us when He sent Jesus to earth to die for us. Jesus' cross was for more than our salvation. Its purpose was for us to become so close to Him that we would experience the joy and peace of living daily in His presence until we live eternally there with Him.

The Tabernacle is a picture of the journey of our hearts as we grow in our relationship with God. It is a picture of Jesus and us, a picture of dying to live. The cross is where it all begins. But now we are to take up our own crosses and carry them to the very end, into the Holy of Holies—the very presence of God—and on into eternity. How much more the words Jesus spoke to His disciples in Matthew 16:24-25 can mean now to anyone who truly desires to be His disciple:

If anyone wishes to come after Me, he must deny himself, and take up his cross and follow Me. For whoever wishes to save his life will lose it; but whoever loses his life for My sake will find it.

FROM THE DOOR TO THE HOLY OF HOLIES

Read now these verses with the purpose of meditating on them. See if they line up with what God desires of us as seen by the diagram of the Tabernacle. Can you see the progression from the Door to the Holy of Holies?

And we know that God causes all things to work together for good to those who love God, to those who are called according to His purpose. For those whom He foreknew, He also predestined to become conformed to the image of His Son, so that He would be the firstborn among many brethren; and these whom He predestined He also called; and these whom He called, He also justified; and these whom He justified, He also glorified (Romans 8:28-30).

And here is a very familiar passage that might have new light now shed on it:

Therefore, brethren, since we have confidence to enter the holy place [the Holy of Holies] *by the blood of Jesus. . .let us draw near with a sincere heart in full assurance of faith, having our hearts sprinkled clean from an evil conscience and our bodies washed with pure water* (Hebrews 10:19,22).

Andrew Murray seems to have a great command of the knowledge we all must discover if we are to take up residence in the Holy of Holies. His words are convicting as well as encouraging. Absorb the truth found here:

Enter into the Holiest. It is a call to the Hebrew to come out of that life of unbelief and sloth, that leads to a departing from the living God, and to enter into the promised land, the rest of God, a life in His fellowship and favour. It is a call to all lukewarm, half-hearted Christians, no longer to remain in the outer court of the Tabernacle, content with the hope that their sins are pardoned. Nor even to be satisfied with having entered the Holy Place, and there doing the service of the Tabernacle, while the veil still hinders the full fellowship with the living God and His love. It calls to enter in through the rent veil, into the place into which the blood has been brought, and where the High Priest lives, there to live and walk and work always in the presence of the Father. It is a call to all doubting, thirsting believers, who long for a better life than they have yet known, to cast aside their doubts, and to believe that this is what Christ has indeed done and brought within the reach of each one of us: He has opened the way into the Holiest! This is the salvation which He has accomplished, and which He lives to apply in each of us, so that we shall indeed dwell in the full light of God's countenance.[7]

Now that you have learned about what our journey is all about, from the Door to the Ark of the Covenant, the next several chapters will show you how it can be accomplished! Prepare to lay your hearts bare!

INTROSPECTION

1. The Holy of Holies is a place of intimacy; Jesus is the Ruler and King of your heart. How are you fixing your eyes on that goal and taking steps to enter into that place?

2. What changes in your daily life will you have to make so that you can die to live?

3. Are you prepared to move from the "what" stage of the Tabernacle's journey into the "how" stage of practical application?

4. Today, how are you carrying your cross through the Tabernacle with the Holy of Holies in sight?

5. You should be able to rightly judge exactly which court you are in. Which one is it?

ENDNOTES

1. Andrew Murray, *The Holiest of All* (New Kensington, PA: Whitaker House, 1996), 244.

2. Murray, *The Holiest of All*, 294.

3. Murray, *The Holiest of All*, 293.

4. Oswald Chambers, *My Utmost for His Highest* (Grand Rapids, MI: Discovery House Publishers, 1963), 73.

5. www.htmlbible.com/sacrednamebiblecom/kjvstrongs/CONHEB805. htm#S8055.

6. Chambers, *My Utmost for His Highest*, 80.

7. Murray, *The Holiest of All*, 353-54.

SECTION TWO

GOD'S COMMANDS

CHAPTER 5

THE CROSSROADS:
CONSIDERING YOUR WAYS

Then the word of the Lord came by Haggai the prophet, saying,
"Is it time for you yourselves to dwell in your paneled houses
while this house lies desolate?" Now therefore, thus says the Lord
of hosts, "Consider your ways!" (Haggai 1:3-5)

Have you ever been on a trip in which it was necessary to read the road map to get where you were going? It was not one of those trips that could be instinctively driven due to familiarity. Traveling from the uncomplicated interstate system to the winding, curvy, country "blue roads" required your skill in map reading, didn't it? The signs along these less-traveled roads usually do not give you all the information you need, so when you came to a four-way stop that presented you with a crossroads, you had to pull out the map to see which direction you were to go in order to reach your final destination. Left? Right? Or straight ahead? This reminds me of a scene at the end of the movie *Cast Away*. Tom Hanks had just returned a FedEx package that had kept him hopeful while he was stranded on an uninhabited island. As he was leaving the ranch where the package had originated, he came to a stop sign on that dirt and gravel road. Looking forward, he contemplated his options. Looking to his left and then his right, he considered again just which direction he would go. Do you get the picture? That is exactly where you stand right now.

Where Are You?

Hopefully, the first four chapters of this book have shown you just where you stand in the Tabernacle of your spiritual journey. Are you contemplating entering the door and stepping into the family of God? Or maybe you are in the Outer Court. Possibly, you have been wandering there for quite awhile, knowing that you are in relationship with Christ because you have believed in Him as Savior and have been baptized, but you haven't begun to take your relationship with Christ seriously yet. Maybe you have entered the Inner Court where you are enjoying walking in the Spirit and eating your daily bread. Your growth in the area of worship is also being developed. Or maybe your walk has taken you to the place where you are standing in front of the veil. Nothing is separating you from the very presence of God now except your own flesh.

Wherever you find yourself on this journey into the Holy of Holies, the question now is where do you want to go? Do you want to stay where you are, move forward, go left, or turn right? You are at a crossroads in your trek to the face of God

As we begin this next section, we will focus on how to apply what we have learned in the first four chapters, what we discovered is essential to our daily walk. It is one thing to have the knowledge to comprehend the symbolism of the Tabernacle, but it is quite another thing to begin to obey the Word of God in such a way that we actually make the journey. Just like the trip described above, we are at a spiritual crossroads. On a real trip, it would never be enough just to know that we are to keep going straight ahead. If we want to reach our destination, we have to move from park to drive, take our foot off of the brake, press on the gas pedal, and proceed with faith in a forward manner, knowing that we are traveling in the right direction. On this spiritual walk, the same is true for us. There is no fruit or reward in standing still. Wherever we are on the path, we must continue in the direction that leads to our further growth in order to reach our goal, the Holy of Holies. We have to take our foot off of the brake that keeps us safe and comfortable. And we have to apply the gas; that is, we have to live out the truth. We must proceed forward in faith!

These next few chapters will be anything but comfortable and safe. Prayerfully, they will challenge you to a new beginning, a new start, on a new kind of journey that is built upon your previous travels. I have a funny little quirk that you might have in common with me. I like to start everything of importance on the first day of the week, the first of the month, or the first of the year. For those of you who wish to continue on this journey, going a little deeper, consider this crossroads as your spiritual January 1 of a brand new millennium, and just for fun, let's make January 1 a Monday as well!

GOD HAS SOMETHING TO SAY

What emotions do you feel about the work that is ahead of you? Are you excited, yet fearful of what is out in front of you? Are you discouraged? Do you feel you should already be farther along than you are? Do you sense the Spirit urging you on, yet you lack the "want to"? Your emotions are valid, but you cannot live by them. They have great potential to steer you wrong. Or you can use them to your advantage! Let's take a look at another Old Testament experience that you might just be able to relate to. Listen to the introduction Kay Arthur gives at the beginning of the Book of Haggai in her *New Inductive Study Bible*. See if you can relate.

> Discouragement reigned. Only a remnant returned to Jerusalem after the 70 years of exile—a small remnant in comparison to the number of people who had been taken captive. Many Jews were reluctant to leave Babylon to return to Jerusalem. The land of their captors had become home. The Babylonians had allowed them to establish businesses and build houses. Their children, while born in captivity, were secure. Why should they leave?
>
> It was a small remnant that returned to rebuild the temple, which soon became a discouraging task. Their zeal had diminished. What began enthusiastically was now being forgotten.

And God's house had not been completed. For about sixteen years the temple stood unfinished and ignored.

Then about 520 b.c., the word of the Lord came to Haggai.[1]

The temple mentioned by Haggai is Solomon's Temple, destroyed when Babylon took Judah into captivity in 586 b.c. It is a very close representation of the Tabernacle of Moses' time that we just studied. Do you see why I thought that the Book of Haggai might be important to us as we learn how to rebuild and take care of our hearts, God's Tabernacle within us? Does the description of this Jewish remnant sound like you as you consider the rebuilding of your heart? Will you become discouraged at the task when the work becomes difficult? Do you know that you have spiritual work to do, but do you lack the zeal to do whatever it takes to make your heart a proper dwelling place for the Spirit? Are you currently experiencing a lack of joy because you have forgotten how to be in God's presence, or have you just never taken the time to learn?

GOD'S MESSAGE: CONSIDER YOUR WAYS!

In this very brief Old Testament book, God will show us some very important things to consider as we seek to obey His call to restore His Tabernacle within us, in our hearts. Let's begin with the first five verses of chapter I. What might we glean from them?

> *In the second year of Darius the king, on the first day of the sixth month, the word of the Lord came by the prophet Haggai to Zerubbabel the son of Shealtiel, governor of Judah, and to Joshua the son of Jehozadak, the high priest, saying, "Thus says the Lord of hosts, 'This people says, "The time has not come, even the time for the house of the Lord to be rebuilt."'" Then the word of the Lord came by Haggai the prophet, saying, "Is it time for you yourselves to dwell in your paneled houses while this house lies desolate? "Now therefore, thus says the Lord of hosts," Consider your ways!"* (Haggai I:1-5)

Zerubbabel the governor and Joshua the priest were the ones who would receive the first two messages that the Lord gave to the prophet Haggai. All three of them were part of the remnant that had returned to Jerusalem from Babylon. The message came to these two because they were the spiritual leaders of the people, and it was the people who decided that it "wasn't time to build the house of the Lord." They were referring to the temple, and the people said this in spite of the fact that God had commanded them to go back and rebuild the temple! These two leaders had done nothing about the people's disobedience to God. In God's second message to them, He challenged their priorities. You can clearly see that the people had been busily building their own *"paneled houses"* while leaving God's house in ruins. And what did God have to say about that? He told them quite plainly to *"Consider* [their] *ways!"*

Doesn't that sound like Christians today? We, too, find ourselves in this hectic and busy world running around like chickens with our heads cut off, doing all the things that make us happy. Our priorities lead us. Our to-do list gives us our marching orders for the day. God has called us to clean out our hearts and make them an appropriate dwelling place for Him, but how much time do we spend with Him, surrendering what lies in ruins inside of us? Our "daily duties" almost always take precedence, don't they? We take care of our physical homes and leave God wondering when we will pay some attention to His home within us. His words to the Jewish remnant are for us today. *"Consider your ways!"* He calls us, even as He called them, to make a dramatic change in our priorities. We must answer the same questions they had to: Will my personal life be a greater priority to me than God is? Will I obey what I know God is asking of me and please Him, or will I feed my flesh and continue doing what pleases me? It's easier to see the flaw in others when they are being disobedient than it is to swallow the bitter pill of the reality of our own disobedience, isn't it? Let's see what else the Lord has to tell the Jews, and us, in the next six verses of Haggai I.

REPERCUSSIONS OF DISOBEDIENCE

"You have sown much, but harvest little; you eat, but there is not enough to be satisfied; you drink, but there is not enough to become drunk; you put on clothing, but no one is warm enough; and he who earns, earns wages to put into a purse with holes." Thus says the Lord of hosts, "Consider your

ways! Go up to the mountains, bring wood and rebuild the temple, that I may be pleased with it and be glorified," says the Lord. "You look for much, but behold, it comes to little; when you bring it home, I blow it away. Why?" declares the Lord of hosts, "Because of My house which lies desolate, while each of you runs to his own house. Therefore, because of you the sky has withheld its dew and the earth has withheld its produce. I called for a drought on the land, on the mountains, on the grain, on the new wine, on the oil, on what the ground produces, on men, on cattle, and on all the labor of your hands" (Haggai 1:6-11).

Is there any doubt in your mind that God delivered consequences to this remnant for their willful disobedience? Do you expect something different from God for your disobedience? What did you find the remnant's consequences to be? What did God allow because of the remnant's wrong priorities? The remnant had worked hard to plant crops to feed their families, but their harvests were small. They had food to eat but not nearly enough to satisfy them. The same occurred with their drink. Though they were not left naked, their clothes were not warm enough. Wages were being earned, but the money didn't go far enough. While they tried to be optimistic, life was consistently coming up short. God's breath seemed to be blowing away every good thing, and the much-needed rains were even being withheld. The land couldn't produce the things that would keep them alive. There seemed to be a drought on everything that touched their lives!

WRONG PRIORITIES

Why was all this happening? Haggai's message from God clearly provided their answer. The drought was all about the remnant's wrong priorities. *"Because of My house which lies desolate, while each of you runs to his own house"* (Hag. 1:9). *"Because of you..."* (Hag. 1:10). Ouch! Their consequences were brought on by their own disobedience in following the plan God had clearly laid out for them.

You might be asking yourself just what this has to do with you and me. I'm glad you are asking! You see, our hearts, God's home, are also lying desolate while we decide whether we can or will be committed enough to finish our journey through the Tabernacle. Our hearts lie in ruins while we continue to walk in our wrong priorities and sinful choices. Anytime we have a lack of commitment and drive to grow and mature in our walk, we are prone to live by those wrong priorities and choices. By the same token, when our priorities are out of whack, they lead us to a lack of commitment to grow and mature and walk toward holiness in God.

Have you desired to drink in the fullness of the Spirit, but He seems to be in short supply? Maybe you have sought after the latest clothing trends while remaining spiritually naked because you have not learned to be clothed in robes of righteousness. Is God the Lord of your finances? If not, how can you expect Him to bless you in them? In our family, our paycheck can disappear quicker than a magician's coin if we don't consider Him the owner of it all. What we gain in one day cannot be retained over the long haul. Have you ever eaten your Sunday lunch and not been able to recall one point of the pastor's message? This is spiritual drought! That happens as a result of a lifestyle of wrong priorities.

When your priorities are focused on you and what you want, you can attend church, sing in the choir, serve at the local mission, and even give your tenth, but there is no real fruit being borne out of these activities. Your "trying" becomes useless to God, and it leaves you unbalanced and dissatisfied with your life. God is just as displeased by our fruitless works as He was with the remnant's fruitlessness, and He certainly is not glorified when we make ourselves the priority.

A SHIFT IN PRIORITIES

God is calling us to consider our ways! But this is not a call just to contemplate the ways in which we are putting ourselves ahead of God. It is a call to action! God didn't stop with the command to "consider your ways" when He gave His message to Haggai to deliver to the remnant. He spoke it twice, and then called them to necessary and obedient action. They would have to get to work on the temple!

> *"Go up to the mountains, bring wood and rebuild the temple, that I may be pleased with it and be glorified," says the Lord* (Haggai 1:8).

God was certainly requiring something of them. They would have to change their focus from themselves and what they wanted to God and what He wanted from them. Today we would call that a change in priorities or a change of heart! Hard work and commitment to the project would also be required if God was to be glorified and pleased.

Are you making the connection? God is asking you to consider your ways, but He isn't about to stop there. He isn't interested in a bunch of people contemplating how wrong they have been to have followed after their own selfish ways. God is interested in those who can see the error of their ways and who desire to change! You see, if you want to walk all the way through the Tabernacle, you eventually will have to leave the ease and comfort of the Outer Court where your salvation and baptism were enough to satisfy you. You will have to make a commitment to change your priorities! Then you will have to realize that walking into the Inner Court (or through the veil into the Holy of Holies) is going to require you to do some hard spiritual work. For God's temple to be restored in you, you will have to go to the mountains and bring down the wood!

Can you imagine how physically difficult it would have been in those days to climb a mountain, cut down many trees, haul the trees back to Jerusalem, strip the trees of their leaves, branches, and bark, and then cut all the wood to the specifications God had for the temple? It seems nearly impossible to me! Yet that was what was required. Does the process of having your heart spiritually restored seem equally impossible to you right now? While there will be some difficult things ahead for you to do, nothing is impossible with God, but He does require something of you! He will ask you to willingly "go to the mountain" and "bring down" what is necessary for your heart to be restored to the heart that He desires.

The remnant had the correct response to their reproof and discipline from God. They joined with the priest and the governor of the land to obey the voice of God, thus reverencing Him, fearing Him with great awe. And God was pleased with them! They had received His rebuke, and then did something about it! How could He not encourage them all the more? *"'I am with you,' declares the Lord"* (Haggai 2:4).

What then should our response be about considering our ways and rebuilding God's temple in our hearts? The remnant is an example to us today. They heard, they obeyed, and they responded with the right actions. We should respond in kind because we love and reverence the Lord our God more than we love our own plans for our lives. To plug our ears and ignore the call of God to "consider our ways" would be willful disobedience.

The chapters that follow will help you to completely understand what it means to "go to the mountains and bring down the wood" by practical spiritual applications. The first step right now, however, is to simply consider your own ways. How have you left God behind? How do you begin the day? How often do you communicate with God? When was the last time you studied your Bible? Do you know where your Bible is?! How have you substituted your own wants for God's desires for you? Look into that heart of yours and do a little spiritual inventory. Record in a notebook what you discover. Then you can use it as a foundation for the work that lies just ahead you.

THE APPLICATION OF TRUTH

Before we leave the Book of Haggai, let's take a brief look at chapter 2. In this chapter, you will be able to find three more significant messages from God to His people. Remember, these messages apply to you as well. They are clearly divided by three repeated phrases: *"The word of the Lord came by Haggai the prophet saying...."* These can be found very easily in verses 1, 10, and 20.

In a nutshell, the messages can be summed up in this way:

1. Don't compare the ruined temple to what it once was (or in our case, don't compare your heart to someone else's). Take courage and don't be discouraged; work! And God will be with you; His Spirit abides with you, so do not fear. He will fill His house (your heart) with His glory. You will experience the peace of God in the temple (in your hearts) (see Haggai 2:1-9).

2. Even though you had not been repentant previously, and you did not bear fruit for God, from now on you will receive His blessing (favor). Consider your own unfaithfulness, but realize He will bless you as you obey (see Haggai 2:10-19).

3. He will overthrow the kingdoms and nations (the gods and sins) that seek to destroy you because He has chosen you. You belong to Him (see Haggai 2:20-23).

Aren't those amazing words from the Lord to us? You don't have to try to make your heart look like anyone else's! If you work toward the goal of a perfected heart, God will fill your heart with His glory and peace! Even though you lacked obedience before and your fruit was rotting on the vine, He will still bless you now as you obey! And the enemy will not be victorious over you because you belong to God. These words from God should encourage you to begin the process of changing your ways. No matter where in the Tabernacle you are standing, you are in the very midst of "Jerusalem," and Jesus is your Governor and High Priest!

This is a simple story, yet it holds wonderful truths for us to digest. Now that you have a little more background, do yourself a huge spiritual favor. . . go back and read Haggai in its entirety! There's more there for you to find!

Let's revisit the applicable truths before we move on. Let them transform your thinking and change your actions. Getting them deeply within your spirit will help you as you delve into the next chapter.

• God and His instructions must become the first priority in our lives (the Word and His teachings) (see Haggai 1:4).

• Our heart, God's Tabernacle, needs repair ahead of our other selfish priorities (see Haggai 1:4).

• God holds back blessings from us when we are walking in disobedience and living with wrong priorities (see Haggai 1:6-11).

• God not only desires for us to "consider our ways," He commands us to! (see Haggai 1:5,7).

- God is pleased and glorified when we finally go to work on our temple (heart) (see Haggai 1:8).

- Our hearts, like the temple, are left desolate because we do what we want to do rather than obey God. Disobedience keeps us from being watered by the Spirit and bearing fruit (see Haggai 1:6,9).

- Obeying what God says in His Word is what shows God that we revere Him (love and fear Him) (see Haggai 1:12).

- When we are obedient children, the Lord stirs up our spirits, making it easier and easier to obey again and again. We think of it backward: "Lord, come and stir my heart so that I can obey You." Obedience precedes stirring (see Haggai 1:14).

- God blesses us when we are obedient to His Word and His priorities (see Haggai 2:19).

Let the Lord bless you as you contemplate now His goodness and faithfulness toward you. God wants to fill your heart with His glory and peace. But He will only do that when you decide to get your priorities straight. When we lay down our selfish, self-absorbed ways that leave us fruitless, then God will begin to overthrow the "kingdoms" that have been trying to overthrow us!

It is time to set your heart and mind on the journey through the Tabernacle. It is God's way to restore your broken and divided heart. It is time for spiritual healing! What are God's priorities for you today, this week, this month, this year? What are your priorities? Do you see where you are standing, right this very moment? You are at a crossroads! Which way will you go?

INTROSPECTION

1. What directives of God have you neglected because you have wrong priorities?

2. What would change in your life if God's priorities became yours?

3. When you are discouraged in your relationship with God, do you tend to quit or persevere?

4. In what way is God's home (your heart) lying desolate because you have not obeyed Him?

5. Will you trust God now to help you overthrow the sin that prevents you from providing Him a great place to dwell?

ENDNOTE

1. Kay Arthur, *The New Inductive Study Bible* (Eugene, OR: Harvest House Publishers, 2000), 1523.

CHAPTER 6

THE "GODS" OF YOUR HEART

Little children, guard yourselves from idols (I John 5:21).

What other gods could we have besides the Lord? Plenty. For Israel there were the Canaanite Baals, those jolly nature gods whose worship was a rampage of gluttony, drunkenness, and ritual prostitution. For us there are still the great gods Sex, Shekels, and Stomach (an unholy trinity constituting one god: self), and the other enslaving trio, Pleasure, Possessions, and Position, whose worship is described as *"The lust of the flesh and the lust of the eyes and the pride of life"* (I John 2:16). Football, the Firm, and Family are also gods for some. Indeed the list of other gods is endless, for anything that anyone allows to run his life becomes his god and the claimants for this prerogative are legion. In the matter of life's basic loyalty, temptation is a many-headed monster.[1]

Gods…the idea of the activity of gods in our lives as believers at first seems ridiculous. After all, God is our God, right? We are going to see in this chapter that we each likely have several gods that enslave us or take us away from our relationship with God. We will see how the Egyptians worshiped false gods and compare that to our own idol worship as we take a very close look at our own hearts. Prepare now to get brutally honest with yourself. But before we delve into the sin and gods in our lives, take a moment to look at what we have just learned. God's message to Israel is His message to us right now.

CONSIDERING YOUR OWN WAYS

In the previous chapter, you learned of the Israeli remnant who returned from their captivity in Babylon with a command from God to rebuild the temple when they arrived back in Jerusalem. When the people responded to the command of God with the disobedience of following after their own priorities, God had a few things to tell them. Haggai's five messages from the Lord to His people can be summed up in just three words: "Consider your ways!"

Have you taken time to process those five messages in light of your own life and set of priorities? God clearly spoke His heart to the Jewish remnant, but He speaks it just as plainly to us in His Word. These messages are transferable truths for us today. Many specific truths can be picked out of them, but let's look at just three in particular.

1. Our hearts are His Tabernacle, the place of His dwelling in us, and He has called us to come out of our slavery and bondage to sin by letting Him work in us. He desires to reconstruct our hearts that are still so full of daily sins. But we must give Him the green light to proceed with His work in us. He is looking for full access to all of our heart, with all its dark nooks and crannies.

2. However, our wrong priorities continually keep us from allowing Him to build in us the temple that He desires our hearts to be.

3. We likely have taken very little time, if any, to evaluate our priorities in this life to see if He is our first priority. Without evaluation of the priorities of our hearts, we will likely never see the kind of heart and life transformation we know is available to us. We will then continue to live out our lives with our own agendas, and we will never experience any

kingdom-impacting change. We will also miss the victory Christ came to give us.

GOD, MOSES, AND THE EGYPTIANS

There is another Old Testament story that will help us see our own wrong priorities. In this chapter, you are going to discover a practical way to identify your wrong priorities, sins, attitudes, and yes, even your "gods." It will be our guide from God's Word and aid us in considering our ways. The story of Moses in Egypt will help you open your eyes to your sin-filled heart. Through this story and another visual aid found at the end of the chapter, you will be able to see what it is that you trust in and rely on instead of the one true God. Think back now on what you know about Moses, Pharaoh, and the ten plagues. Let me refresh your memory.

God told Moses that he was going to go face to face and toe to toe with Pharaoh, the Egyptian leader of the land. God promised that if Moses would obey Him by publically proclaiming all that He had commanded him, then He would take care of Pharaoh. God also would be faithful to bring Israel out of the bondage they had been held in for 430 years. Great judgments would come upon Pharaoh and the Egyptians, and from these great signs and wonders, the Egyptians would know that the God of Israel was the only God. God's plan was not just to set His people free. You see, God wanted Israel's Egyptian captors to have a chance to know Him as *Yahweh* as well, a name of God that had just been revealed to Israel. God was as interested in their hearts as He was in the hearts of His chosen children, the Israelites. And here's an important fact for us to always remember: God is just as interested in mine and yours! God wanted to show the Egyptians (and us!) what He wanted them to know about idol worship—that He is opposed to it and desires our God-worship!

The Egyptians were definitely engaged in "god" worship. When God sent the ten plagues, each one of them was aimed at particular Egyptian gods, not Pharaoh and Egypt itself. The plagues were designed to show that *Yahweh* was the one and only Supreme God. All of the Egyptians witnessed the gruesome plagues and were shown very precisely that not one of their gods had answered their cries. Their "gods" had been strangely silent and predictably inactive!

GOD OVERCOMES THE GODS OF THE EGYPTIANS

In searching out the gods of the Egyptians, I quickly found out how pervasive idol worship was in that society. But what amazed me the most was God's great proficiency in putting their "gods" to shame. Let's look at each individual plague and see what God was really doing through them.

According to the chart on the "gods" in *Nelson's Complete Book of Bible Maps and Charts*, God prevailed over at least this many of the Egyptian "gods," and likely many more. The plague is listed, then the "gods" over which our God prevailed.

1. The Nile turned to blood—prevailing over two gods of the Nile

2. The frogs—prevailing over a crude primordial goddess symbolized by a frog

3. Lice—prevailing over the goddess of healing

4. Swarm of insects—prevailing over two earth gods and a god of the harvest

5. Death of livestock—prevailing over two gods (ruler and guardian of life) and the creature god

6. Boils—prevailing over the goddesses of healing and sickness and the creature god

7. Hail—prevailing over two sky gods, two sky goddesses, god of death, life, and vegetation, guardian of life, god of storms and crops, and god of the harvest

8. Locusts—prevailing over three gods of vegetation, crops, and harvest and three earth gods

9. Darkness—prevailing over the gods of sun, rising sun, and eye of the sun, two gods of Egypt, and a god of the sun and sky

10. Death of the firstborn—prevailing over three death gods, creature god, goddess of life and healing, god of justice, protector of newborns and destiny, god of sickness, guardian of life, god of chaos, god of fate, and god of women in labor.[2]

Do you see what God did? He progressively put their own gods under a microscope for the Egyptians to see! Do you remember reading of any response from these "gods" in the story? They never came to the rescue. And why not? Because they really weren't God! They were imposters, false gods, who were created in the hearts of the men who trusted in them. They weren't real!

OUR GODS

When I initially studied all of these gods in this story in light of the God of the Bible, I wondered how God wanted me to practically apply in my own life what He had just shown me. You might be wondering the same thing right about now.

Here is what God spoke to me in answer to my question: "I want to be the *Lord*—*Yahweh*—over all of your false gods."

Did I have any false gods residing in my heart? Do you? Have I created, trusted in, and relied on any other god but the Lord? Have you? What just came to your mind? Was it a sinful action? Was it a personal character trait?

Look back over the ten plagues and the gods that the plagues exposed. Don't the Egyptian gods seem blatantly false, and therefore not real? Why weren't they able to see that their gods—not one of them—came to their aid? Why didn't they see what God was doing and listen to His voice?

But our gods don't seem to be so blatantly false, do they? Maybe you are even thinking, "I don't worship any gods." Do you think that god-worship is having a physical idol in your home on your mantle that you bow down to, like Buddha? Check your heart again. I have heard it said that today's idols are more in the self than on the shelf!

Do you need to be in control of everything (or anything)? Do you need to be number one? Do you seek to be noticed? Do you have an addiction to food, cigarettes, alcohol, drugs, sex, or pornography? Maybe your addiction is to your day-timer, cell phone, texting, computer and its games, Facebook, television, movies, video games, work, ministry, children's activities, sports, or money and shopping. Maybe your gods look more like: selfishness, lying to impress others, jealousy of what others have that you don't, hatred masked by proclaiming you just don't care for a particular person, gossiping, judgment, coarse talk and joking, "pot-stirring," thinking that no one can do things better than you, unforgiveness, etc.!

A god in your heart is anything you are unwilling to let go of. It is something you trust in and rely on rather than God. It is anything that you spend too much time with at the expense of your relationship with God or the priorities He has for you. Think of the story of the rich young man in Matthew 19:16-26. The young man came to Jesus wanting to know what other good thing he might do to obtain eternal life. Jesus' answer for him was simply to *"keep the commandments."* The young man avowed that he had kept these commandments. What Jesus said in reply is as important for us as it was for the young man. Jesus said:

> *If you wish to be complete, go and sell your possessions and give to the poor, and you will have treasure in heaven; and come, follow Me* (Matthew 19:21).

You see, Jesus could see right into the young man's heart. He knew that there was something that he was hanging on to, trusting in more than he trusted in Him. For this man, it was his money. What is it for you?

Our completion (perfection, growth in the Lord, maturity) is dependent upon discovering what those things are that we rely on "in a pinch." These are the very things that are preventing us from walking in the Spirit. Once He helps us to identify them, He will ask us to do the same thing that He required of the rich young man. He will ask us to give them up! And the only way to do that is to *"come, follow [Him]."* The rich young man had a choice to make, and he didn't choose wisely. Shortly, you will be faced with the same type of choices. Will you lay down your gods and follow after the one and only God? Will you be honest with yourself and say what Isaiah said of himself and the Israelites? He said this in Isaiah 26:13: *"O Lord our God, other masters besides You have ruled us."*

Or will you continue in a lifestyle that leads to a predictable legacy for your children and grandchildren found in Second Kings 17:41 that says:

> *So while these nations feared the Lord, they also served their idols; their children likewise and their grandchildren, as their fathers did, so they do to this day.*

GOD WANTS WHAT IS IN OUR HEARTS

Can you see that it is not enough to merely fear the Lord if we are going to continue to serve those idols in our life that take precedence over our reverence of and service to God? That will lead to a spiritual legacy that is undesirable to think about. It is important for us to question ourselves as to just how long we will allow ourselves to walk in sin and idol worship. We must consider, at some point in our journey toward the very face of God, our need to put our flesh to death even as Christ suffered in His flesh. It is the only way that we will be able to walk in the Spirit. The Lord told us this more eloquently in First Peter 4:1-3. Absorb its truth, especially the last sentence. This is a verse that has helped me tremendously as I have striven to remove idols and sin from my own heart.

> *Therefore, since Christ has suffered in the flesh, arm yourselves also with the same purpose, because he who has suffered in the flesh has ceased from sin, so as to live the rest of the time in the flesh no longer for the lusts of men, but for*

the will of God. For the time already past is sufficient for you to have carried out the desire of the Gentiles, having pursued a course of sensuality, lusts, drunkenness, carousing, drinking parties and abominable idolatries.

God's point to us is simple and clear: Enough time has already passed in our lives that we have lived with a divided and spiritually unhealthy heart. We have spent plenty of time already pursuing those things that divide our heart because they are more important to us than He is! So we must ask ourselves, "When is enough, enough?"

God wants to be Lord over those priorities that are elevated above Him. He wants our sins that we have refused to bring to Him in repentance. He wants those wrong attitudes that we continue to call our "personality." He wants our surrender, the same kind of surrender that He required of the rich young man, and that ultimately was required of Him. He wants to overcome in us everything that we do, think, or say that is not scripturally correct or aligned with His holiness.

I love how Oswald Chambers put it:

> The only way we can be of use to God is to let Him take us through the crooks and crannies of our own characters. It is astounding how ignorant we are about ourselves! We do not know envy when we see it, or laziness, or pride. Jesus reveals to us all that this body has been harboring before His grace began to work. How many of us have learned to look in with courage?[3]

THE DIAGRAM OF YOUR HEART

Glance at the heart included at the end of this chapter. It is a representation of a typical heart of any person, Christian or not. Every one of us has at least one major breach in our heart, something that allowed the entrance of the enemy into our young hearts. The breach will be as different as each of us, particular to our own life and experience. A breach is often an emotionally damaging, traumatic event. The jagged pieces of your heart will be the sin or gods in your life that have grown up in you as a result of the breach. Begin by prayerfully determining what your major breach is, for it will reveal what your gods are. Each god is the direct result of a lie that you believed because of the breach. Fill each compartment of the diagram of the heart with a sin, attitude, or disposition, a god that you let rule your life. This will help you get an accurate picture of what your heart looks like. As painful as this might be for you to see, this is the heart that God sees. But the good news is that He wants to perfect it in you, and He is able to do just that!

What do you see in those pieces? Don't get hung up on filling ten spaces. Some people only fill a few because that is all that they see at the time. Others have divided each of the ten chambers in half and filled twenty spaces, and it still wasn't enough. The point is this: you need to pray for direction from the Spirit and fill up your heart as He directs and leads. And He will lead you to fill it with your "stuff," the stuff you rely on and trust in to get you by—just like the Egyptians.

Do you feel convicted right now? You are not alone. Let me share with you a little of what God spoke to me when He first showed me this heart and what I was supposed to do with it. And then I will share my personal heart assignment with you.

THE STORY OF MY HEART

After God had me draw this very ugly heart, He said to me, "You have stuff hidden in the creases of your heart. What has been clearly noticeable as sin, you have let Me work on. But what remains are these. They are your sinful attitudes, and they are deeply rooted in your heart. Each of them is a god of your own making. You have trusted in them in a thousand different moments when you weren't trusting in Me. Each one must be recognized, confessed, surrendered to Me, and crucified."

God spoke so plainly to me about what was in my heart, and I knew He definitely wanted me to respond in the way He had described to me. But the choice would be up to me. Would I recognize the sin and not rationalize why it was there? Would I confess it, vowing to turn away from it by my true repentance? Would I really surrender each sinful part to Him? Pharaoh hardened his heart ten times. Would I choose to have a

Pharaoh-like attitude that resulted in an unchanged and hardened heart, or would I choose to be Christlike, surrendering my heart to God so that He could transform it?

Allow me now to reveal to you my sin. Trust me; this is not easy, because pride would prefer to keep it all hidden. Pride wonders what you will think of me if you know the real me. God has already had me share this with my women's group at church and with the small group I lead in my home. But sharing this with you won't be any easier simply because of previous disclosure. In fact, it is much more difficult for me because you are people of unknown numbers whom I do not know. But I am trusting that God will be glorified as I once again crucify my flesh, all my natural tendencies toward sin, and dependence on something other than God. May my testimony be a blessing to you as you allow God to search out your heart and fill in your spaces. Now let me be very transparent with you. Here is what God showed me about my heart. Hopefully it will help you be honest with yourself about your own sin-stained heart.

Let me begin with the breach. I had not only one major breach in my heart, but a second one as well. These breaches formed a different heart in me than the one God intended for me when He created me in my mother's womb. Once my heart had been broken, it could now hear the lies of an enemy who intended to destroy any faith in God that might have been developing in me. These tears in my heart left me vulnerable to satan's attacks. But the most destructive thing these breaches were responsible for were my many rationalizations and justifications of why I was the way I was. My breaches became, for a while, my excuses to be sinful in my attitudes and actions.

My first breach occurred when I was about two years old. Yes, wounds of the heart can occur from birth, even in infants. When I was two, my parents began to have struggles that were threatening their relationship. Because of the wounds that were being inflicted upon my mother's heart, she unknowingly and unintentionally withdrew her emotional connection to me while she tried to take care of her own breaking heart. It was what she knew to do. But that emotional desertion left my heart torn and bleeding. As a two-year-old, I had no ability to reconnect by joining myself back together with my mom. I don't remember it even happening. This disconnection became my "normal."

My second breach took place throughout the rest of my childhood. This breach had several offshoots, but it can be summed up by this: the destruction of my family. This included an alcoholic father, physical abuse within our home (but not to me or my brothers), and divorce.

These realities of my family caused me much shame and heartache. Initially, they played out in my teen years as perfectionism and the "good girl" syndrome. But the first breach had a devastating effect on my emotional growth, and I learned to stuff all of my emotions. I rarely ever shed tears and almost never publicly. I didn't want anyone to know what I was experiencing. The saying, "No man is an island; no man stands alone," was never true for me. I was an island, and I preferred to stand alone.

As a Christian adult, I began to wonder why I was not spiritually growing. It had to do with several things, but I have come to the realization that the main reason was because I had a sin-filled heart, and I didn't even realize it. The "good girl" façade couldn't cover my sin any longer. My Holy God would not allow me to go any further without a complete heart transformation. His way of taking me all the way through to heart healing was to give me this lesson from Pharaoh and this simple diagram of a broken and shattered heart.

The first time that I drew out this heart according to God's directions, it looked so ugly to me. The jagged edges of its brokenness told the story of my life. But it was only when the Holy Spirit began to show me the words that defined my gods that I could see the real ugliness in me. These are the words that filled my divided heart: emotional disconnectedness, self-sufficiency, self-elevation, selfishness, judgmental, defensiveness, hatred/anger, control, an opinion on everything, and self-righteousness. Do you see what I mean by ugly?

Staring at my broken heart, I realized that I had spent years covering these things up with the rationalization of my breaches. They were hidden beneath the foreskin of my heart, in its deep crevices. But now my childhood experiences could no longer be my excuse. Jesus had died for the remission of these sins, yet they had remained with me. Now they would have to go, but how? I had tried on my own to eradicate my sins by sheer willpower, but I had never succeeded—ever! I am not a proponent of New Year's resolutions for just that very reason. My flesh was never able to transform my ugly heart. I knew that it would only happen if God transformed me by giving me a circumcised heart.

God began to show me how much my heart looked like Pharaoh's hardened heart. As he had trusted in so many other gods, these words written on the chambers of my heart revealed to me exactly what my gods were. They were those attitudes and dispositions I had trusted in to get me through everything that came my way. I leaned on them when life was not going as I intended. They ruled my life. God could not be called my Lord when I defaulted to my fleshly heart attitudes. They were.

As I began to take out this heart every day and pray over it, I was struck by one thought. Every one of my sins was rooted in my own pride and self-absorption. One day as I was surrendering my "heart" to God, I got out a highlighter and wrote the word "pride" across my heart in bold capital letters. And that is when it hit me. At the core of my heart diagram was one letter, the letter "I." I was keeping me from being transparent. I was keeping myself from getting closer to God and others. I was just like Pharaoh. I was the center of my life!

Now I needed to know from the Lord just how I could change my heart and put it back together again. I wanted a united heart, one that was unbroken and complete. Deep inside me I knew that I wanted my heart to be healed, once and for all. I desperately wanted to keep it from growing harder and colder. The Lord told me very precisely that the process of sanctification was the only way to have an unbroken heart. He reminded me that the Inner Court of the Tabernacle was the place where that would begin to take place. Do you remember it? It is the place where we partake of the Word every day as if our very life depended upon it, where the Holy Spirit illuminates truth to us in ways that are fresh and new, and where we stand before the presence of God and worship Him in Spirit and in truth! It is where our flesh, our pride, is crucified!

So every day, bit by bit, I brought my heart before the Lord. Some days I prayed over all ten gods written in the broken chambers. Other days just one or two of them would leap off of the paper, and I would pray over them. And then, as I saw progress in my actions and words, I began to thinly highlight in yellow inside the space where I had witnessed growth. As the spaces slowly began to fill in (some more quickly than others), I realized that transformation was happening, but I wasn't doing it! I hadn't set out to change myself. I had embarked on a journey to be changed, and the Holy Spirit was fulfilling His call in me! As I continued to lay my heart before Him, confessing and surrendering each individual god, my broken, bleeding, and jagged heart was becoming a united and restored heart, and it was being knit back together by the Spirit. My heart, which a few weeks earlier looked like Pharaoh's, was now looking much more like Christ's, and my attitudes and actions reflected that change.

So what led me to initially draw out such a heart? The Spirit's inspiration and the Word of God opened my eyes to it. Look with me at the verse God gave me that created in my mind the picture of the broken heart.

> *Teach me Your way, O Lord; I will walk in Your truth; unite my heart to fear Your name* (Psalm 86:11).

Awesome, isn't it? God knows that our hearts, even after salvation, are broken and divided. The apostle Paul obviously knew it as well, for that is the very thing he talks about in Romans 7:15-21. He can't seem to understand why, when he wants to do the right things, he continually does the wrong things. He needed the Lord, just as we do, to unite the pieces of our hearts. God alone is capable of healing them. When we finally see our broken hearts being restored by the Spirit of God, we will be able to become all that He intends us to be—like Him. This is sanctification. This is the highway to holiness.

PHARAOH'S POOR EXAMPLE

We must be careful, though, of our response to God's revelation of the gods found in our hearts. Remember, Pharaoh was shown the sin of his idol worship with each of the ten plagues sent by God. Pharaoh's response was a hardened heart toward the God who sent the plagues. With each plague, his heart was hardened all the more. But when you look at the biblical account of this story, we can see some other responses as well. Be careful as you work through your own "heart." Keep referring back to this list, making sure that you are not responding to the Holy Spirit as did Pharaoh.

- Pharaoh begged relief from the consequences of trusting other gods.

God might not remove the natural consequences of our sin and idol worship. We should beg Him to change our hearts, not the consequences of our sin.

- Pharaoh made promises that he never intended to keep. Once the pressure was off, he seemed to forget the promises he made.

Don't make promises to God that you do not intend to keep. God is a covenant-keeping God, and He takes vows and promises very seriously.

- Pharaoh refused to listen to reason. When his people pleaded with him not to continue making the God of the Israelites mad, he refused the advice.

How are you responding to the things God is sharing with you through this study? Refusing His counsel to you means that you will likely keep worshipping your idols.

- Pharaoh tried to bargain his way out of a plague by offering Moses something other than what God told Moses he would receive.

Trying to bargain with God by only partially putting away an idol, or telling God that you will take care of it sometime soon (so you don't have to lay it down today), will lead you deeper into that idolatry and further away from God.

- Pharaoh had a revelation about God and his own sinfulness, but he never had a heart change.

Be careful not to walk away from reading this, having a new revelation or new insight, and then forget what the most important result is to be: Getting your idols out of your heart and into God's hands. Heart transformation!

God is patient with us, like He was with Pharaoh, but He won't allow us to continue in our sin and the worship of other gods. Think about just one thing that God has revealed to you that belongs in the diagram of your heart. Now say this to yourself: How has *(my idol)* ever helped me? When I need help, isn't *(my idol)* strangely silent, even as the Egyptian gods were?

PRAYING OVER YOUR HEART

Are you serious about getting the gods of your life into the hands of Almighty God? If you are, here is how you can do that. Draw a heart on an 8.5 by 11-inch sheet of paper. Make it similar to the one found in this chapter. Plan a time when you can be alone with God for a good length of time—an hour would be great. Humble yourself before God by getting down on your knees. Begin to ask the Holy Spirit to bring to your mind the idols of worship that can be found in your heart. They might be attitudes (like most of mine were) or behaviors. Your heart won't look like mine. It will look like you.

As the Spirit brings something to mind, write it in one of the spaces. Stop when the Spirit stops revealing things to you. If you have more than ten, then add them on a list on the side of the heart or just divide your heart into more than ten chambers. Make a new heart sheet if you'd like. Now, ask the Spirit to reveal to you what the very first breach of your heart was. Be open to let Him show you more than one. Write them in the area of the crevasse of the heart. Begin to pray over each one of the idols, including your breach. Confess them to God and share with Him how you have seen them played out in your life. Surrender your heart to Him for His transformation, over and over, day after day, patiently and with great humility.

You might want to share your "heart" with someone. Be accountable to that person by letting them know how you are praying daily. Let them know of any changes and transformations you have observed. Let them encourage you in the work that God is doing in you. (It is very difficult to daily look upon the sin in your heart. Encouragement along the way was tremendously helpful to me.)

Every day, bring your heart to God and pray over it, asking Him to repair it for you. Ask Him to help you see where changes are occurring, and record the changes you experience by filling that space with a thin line of highlighter (it will take awhile to completely fill the space). The goal is to fill the holes in your heart with the highlighter, the "light" of God! This will help you see your own progress, and it is a motivator for even greater change.

When you completely fill your heart with highlighter, make a new heart and repeat the process. Hopefully some of the "gods" will be dead to you. But I am positive that God will give you more insights regarding other gods that you can fill in the spaces. Sanctification is a life-long process!

Think back with me now to the Tabernacle. Each piece of our heart—each god and each sin—must be taken from the door to the Holy of Holies. Each piece must be covered with the blood of the Sacrificial Lamb. Realize that *"there is now no condemnation"* (Rom. 8:1). Each piece of your heart must be baptized with God's cleansing. Realize that *"though your sins are as scarlet, they will be as white as snow."* Each piece must be taken to the workbench in the Inner Court where it can be illuminated by the Spirit, changed by the Word of God, and transformed by your true spiritual worship of the one and only God—your obedience to Him and His Word! This is where our hearts are restored, rebuilt, united, and healed. This is when your heart becomes Christlike. This is the crucifying of your flesh that prepares you for the Holy of Holies—seeing God face to face! What a marvelous way for God to spiritually cleanse and sew up the ragged edges of our sin-filled hearts.

SAFEGUARDING YOUR HEART

One final note—First Peter 2:9 teaches us that we are part of God's royal priesthood. It is the priest's job to "keep charge" of the Tabernacle according to Numbers 1:47-54. The Hebrew rendering of "keep charge" is this: preserve, keep safe, safeguard, take custody of, and serve as if on sentry patrol. Are you keeping charge of your heart? Will you? Will you offer up your broken heart to God and allow Him to heal you? God already knows everything there is to find in your heart, so nothing is going to shock Him. Psalm 44:20-21 says this:

> *If we had forgotten the name of our God, or extended our hands to a strange god, would not God find this out? For He knows the secrets of the heart.*

And be reminded from Psalm 78:8 that there is a generation who is *"stubborn and rebellious...a generation that did not prepare its heart* [put it right], *and whose spirit was not faithful to God."* Do you belong to the generation that desires to put their hearts right with God, or will you remain in your stubborn rebellion? The latter will make you like Pharaoh. The former will make you like Christ.

THE REST OF MY STORY

I have a couple of notes of encouragement for you. First, on a personal note, my relationship with my mother is being restored even as I write this. There is only one way to restore emotional connectedness between two people who have been emotionally separated for 48 years—by the Holy Spirit, the Word of God, and a lot of repentant prayer! I praise God for His miracle that He is doing in both of us! The second note of encouragement comes from Oswald Chambers. He tells us this: "There is no heaven with a little corner of hell in it. God is determined to make you pure and holy and right."[4]

Let God's words encourage you as well. Paul eloquently speaks to us on this very process.

Or what agreement has the temple of God with idols? For we are the temple of the Living God...."Come out from their midst and be separate"...let us cleanse ourselves from all defilement of flesh and spirit, perfecting holiness in the fear of God (2 Corinthians 6:16-17; 7:1).

God desires for you to "go up to the breaches" and "build a wall around" the house of God, our hearts. By giving Him access to your heart to close the breach and destroy your idols, He is able to repair and restore your heart with a strong wall that will protect it in the future. Whitewashing or trying to plaster over your damaged heart will never mend it. Only God can do that through you. (See Ezekiel 13:5,10-14.) It is time to begin to consider the members of your body as dead to all forms of sin, for that is idolatry (see Col. 3:5).

Be very encouraged. God is not through with you yet, if you are willing to walk on!

INTROSPECTION

1. What are the gods and sin of your heart that are hidden in its creases? If you haven't already, draw a copy of the broken heart that can be found on page 129. Fill it in with the gods and sins that the Lord has revealed to you.

2. Contemplate the ways in which you have trusted in them instead of God. How have you used them to "get you through," instead of relying on God and praying through your need?

3. How have you rationalized that these have been helpful to you?

4. Christlikeness will be the result of the process of sanctification, removing the gods and sin, bit by bit, from your heart where He resides in the form of the Holy Spirit. Prayer over these issues is the power for the victory over them. How important is it to you to pray every day over your sin- and god-filled heart?

5. Prayer is the beginning of surrender, and surrender leads to the spiritual healing of your broken heart. Are you willing to do what it takes to see that goal realized?

ENDNOTES

1. James Packer, *Your Father Loves You* (Harold Shaw Publishers, 1986), www. sermonillustrations.com/a-z/i/idolatry.htm.

2. *Nelson's Complete Book of Bible Maps and Charts* (Nashville, TN: Thomas Nelson Publishers, 1993), 25-28.

3. Oswald Chambers, *My Utmost for His Highest* (Grand Rapids, MI: Discovery House Publishers, 1963), 12.

4. Chambers, *My Utmost for His Highest,* 183.

CHAPTER 7

TAKE FULL VENGEANCE!

But may it never be that I would boast, except in the cross of our Lord Jesus Christ, through which the world has been crucified to me, and I to the world (Galatians 6:14).

Did you take the challenge? Did you fill in the diagram of the broken heart with the gods, sins, and ungodly attitudes of your own life? Have you been praying over it, trusting God to unite your heart as He has always intended it to be?

Now that you have allowed the Holy Spirit to illuminate your real heart, and you have seen the sin that still remains, it is critical that you find a way to apply God's truth so that you can overcome the besetting sins of your life.

We used the Old Testament story of Moses and Pharaoh to help us identify the sin in our fractured hearts. Now let's look at another part of Moses' story, the story of the Israelites' venture into the Promised Land. It will help us to understand the importance of destroying the sin of our hearts. Our story is found in Numbers 31, but before we go there, let's think back on the story of Moses and God's people leaving Egypt and its bondages.

GOD'S PROMISE AND COMMAND

In Exodus 20, after the Ten Commandments had been given to Moses, and the Israelites were on their way to the Promised Land, God spoke these words to His servant Moses:

You shall not make other gods besides Me; gods of silver or gods of gold, you shall not make for yourselves (Exodus 20:23).

Even before the plagues had come upon Egypt and Pharaoh, God plainly and with great love for His chosen said this to Moses regarding the Israelites:

I also established My covenant with them, to give them the land of Canaan, the land in which they sojourned. . . .I will bring you to the land which I swore to give to Abraham, Isaac, and Jacob, and I will give it to you for a possession (Exodus 6:4,8).

Both the promise of a land to be given to them and the command to only worship and obey Him were critical to the success of God's plan for His people. God intended for His promise and their obedience to be inseparable. But they, like us, were much more prone to focus on the promise and totally forget the command. So when the Israelites stood on the banks of the Jordan River, ready to step into the Promised Land, they assumed that God would do all the work of destroying their enemies who occupied the land given to them. Then they could live there forever, blessed by the God who loved them so much. Having long since forgotten the command to worship no other gods but God, this chosen people entered the land, experienced some military victories by taking over the land, and settled in to live their lives in this place that was their new home. They became complacent and did not finish the work that God had called them to do—to drive out all of the inhabitants of the land. And they became friendly and quite comfortable with the very people they were told to drive out. Unfortunately, they also began to worship some of the gods of their newfound friends and neighbors.

Listen to the strong words of God to Moses, their spiritual and military leader:

Take full vengeance for the sons of Israel on the Midianites; afterward you will be gathered to your people (Numbers 31:2).

On this side of the Jordan, before God's people would cross over, He gave Moses one last opportunity to lead his people to obedience to the Lord, their God. They had a terrible track record of disobeying God's commands, and there would be no other chances to influence this obstinate, stiff-necked people. So, Moses spoke to the Israelites, telling them of God's latest command.

The Lure of the Midianites

We must ask ourselves the question, "What is the reason that God wanted His children to take full vengeance on the Midianites?" What had happened to move God to direct them in this way? We only have to look back a few chapters to see why it would be imperative to follow this command of God. The answers to our questions can be found in Numbers 25.

God wanted Israel to take full vengeance on the Midianites for a very good reason. The Israelites had broken the very first commandment that God had given them when they were lured into the worship of the Midianite gods. Here is the commandment they ignored:

You shall have no other gods before Me....You shall not worship them or serve them; for I, the Lord your God, am a jealous God..." (Exodus 20:3,5).

Israel had joined in the Midianite and Moabite worship of Baal while on their way to the Promised Land. God pronounced a plague that would kill everyone who worshiped Baal. One man was bold enough to take a Midianite woman, in the sight of Moses and all of Israel, and attempt to sleep with her. After he and the woman were killed by Phinehas the priest for the man's disobedience to God's command, then another 24,000 Israelites died in a plague for their own willful idol worship (see Numbers 25:1-9).

Now, it was God's turn. In chapter 31, we hear His call for vengeance to come upon those people who were using their gods and customs to turn God's people away from Him. God was primed to take full vengeance on the Midianites for leading His people astray.

We have a hard time understanding that, don't we? We like to think of God as forgiving and gracious toward us. As believers, He is. But He wants anything that turns our hearts from Him to be destroyed. When it comes to the worship of any other god but Him, God has a zero tolerance policy for every person who calls Him their God! God wanted the Midianites to be physically destroyed so that they could not spiritually destroy His children. But He also wanted those dear children of His to see and know the consequences of their own disobedient idol worship. Their willful disobedience to His commands cost them 24,000 of their own people.

God could have easily destroyed the Midianites with His armies from Heaven. Instead, He called the Israelites to execute His judgment (verse 3). There was something to be learned in not being "delivered" by the arm of God. God would surely be with them to accomplish this task, but they were responsible to carry out the Lord's vengeance. God wasn't asking for a war where some would die for leading Israel astray. God required that the Midianites must come to a full end because of their gods and idol worship. He also did not want His perfect plan for the purity of His chosen to be maligned by these people who worshiped their own false gods.

ISRAEL'S DISOBEDIENCE

God gave Israel His plan for the destruction of the Midianites: they were to choose 12,000 armed men to go to war against the Midianites, 1,000 military men from each of the 12 tribes. Each tribe stood to lose the same number of men when they went to war. These men then set out to go to war against the five kings of Midian. They knew their "marching orders" well. They were to kill everyone and everything, for that was what God meant by full vengeance. There was no question as to what God required of them, and no other options!

So these 12,000 men of war set out to destroy all of the Midianites. Even Phinehas the priest went out with them to be God's agent for them, for he carried with him the holy vessels and the trumpets for alarm in his hand. They wouldn't lose—they couldn't lose! Just as the Lord had commanded them, they went to war and killed all of the men and the kings with the sword. They captured the women and the children. Then they took all their cattle and all their flocks . . .

What did they do? Did these 12,000 soldiers obey God? Did they comply with God's command? Had not God said to them, *"Take full vengeance"*? Do you see what they did? They disobeyed the command of their God. They killed the men and kings but captured the women, kept them alive, and plundered the animals, too! Why would they do that? They had been sent into battle because the Midianites were idol worshipers instead of God-worshipers. God wanted to teach His children to obey while keeping them pure, and yet they disobeyed again!

Let's just process that a little bit. No one can say for sure exactly why they disobeyed, but being part of the human race, we might be able to come up with at least a few possibilities, given their past record of disobedient behavior.

1. The Israelite men had a thing for the Midianite women—any women, for that matter! It had been the Midianite women who had brought these men into sin by introducing their gods to them. The men then married these women who were outside of the Jewish faith, thus destroying the purity and holy calling of the Jewish race.

2. They did not want to destroy what their flesh definitely wanted to hang on to and enjoy—the women.

3. They wanted to be in control instead of allowing God to be in charge. Flesh doesn't normally like to be told what to do by God or anyone else.

4. Maybe they thought God would somehow be pleased with them for keeping the women and children alive. He might just approve of their compassion.

Can't you just see them merrily returning to camp with those they took captive and all the spoils, hoping to be rewarded for the fine work they had accomplished and for the wealth they were bringing into the family? They were surely proud of their increase, and they probably couldn't wait to choose from the booty what would be their reward for a job well done.

No matter what the reason for their disobedience, the truth is that they still disobeyed God, and He and Moses would surely have something to say about that! Moses was angry! Surely his words to them cut them to the quick! There was no applause, no congratulations, no heroes' welcome home from battle. This is what Moses said to them:

> *Have you spared all the women? Behold, these caused the sons of Israel...to trespass against the Lord...so the plague was among the congregation of the Lord* (Numbers 31:15-16).

So we can get a better idea of what was really being said here, let's take a closer look at the word "spared." It literally means "let live," but looking at a Hebrew dictionary to more clearly define this word as it is used in this context, it means this:

1. To revive

2. To keep, leave, or make alive

3. To give life to

4. To nourish (feed)

5. To preserve

6. To repair or restore to life.

You might be asking yourself, "So...?" I agree that it is not all that interesting, unless you apply those definitions to yourself and your gods! Think back on the heart assignment from the previous chapter. Let's compare that chapter to the story in this chapter.

OUR RESPONSE TO THE GODS IN OUR LIVES

God originally called Israel to take full vengeance on the Midianites because of their sinful influence on Israel and because they brought their gods into the everyday life of Israel. Now what do you think God wants you to do with your heart that is filled with the gods you have identified? He wants *you* to take full vengeance on them! Why? For the exact same reasons that He commanded Israel to take full vengeance on the Midianites. Look at how the application matches!

1. God knows that our gods are a threat to our holiness and purity, just like the gods of the Midianites led to Israel's impurity. They affect our relationship with God, building thrones in our hearts from where they rule us. They become our master to the point that Jesus cannot be our Lord.

2. God knows that we tend to like to keep those things around us that gratify our flesh. He knows that our gods feed our sinful nature that has been crucified with Christ; thus, our sinful nature that Christ declares is dead in us is being revived in us. What we have been given clear victory over, we surrender into the hands of our enemy.

3. God knows that He is the only one who can be in control of our lives if He is going to be able to lead us to holiness. Yet, we continue to let our fleshly desires control all of us.

4. God knows that our gods will never please Him, and they usually bring disaster upon us.

We are destined to be disciplined just as these Israelite soldiers were if we disobey as they did. We, too, can no longer allow our idols and gods to be spared when we have been commanded to take full vengeance on them. The soldiers let their enemy off the hook when they spared the women. We let our enemy off the hook when we refuse to annihilate the gods that take our eyes off of God. We also can't allow our idols to be worshiped alongside of God. Remember, He is a jealous God who demands that *He* be our only God. This double-mindedness is surely observed by unbelievers who need salvation. When they see our double-mindedness, they see us as the hypocrites that we truly are, for we look like them, like the world. Consider carefully some insights recorded in my journal that I gained from Micah 4 that seem to align themselves with this thought.

Many nations will come and say, "Come and let us go up to the mountain of the Lord and to the house of the God of Jacob, that He may teach us about His ways and that we may walk in His paths."...Though all the peoples walk each in the name of his god, as for us, we will walk in the name of the Lord our God forever and ever (Micah 4:2,5).

Those verses prompted me to record this in my journal:

All Christians have a "walk." We all show up on Sundays at the mountain we call church to be taught about His ways, and the desired result is that the teaching will have an impact on the "walk" we are currently experiencing (see Micah 4:2). We are being taught for one purpose—that we may walk in His paths! Yet the true testimony of so many believers today is that we have been taught and taught and taught! We could teach seminary classes on what we have learned and know. But the rest of our testimony is often that, though we know a lot, we continue to walk in the name of our "gods" rather than in the name of the one and only true God. We know what we know, but we walk in our flesh (see Micah 4:5). So, we basically are worshiping our gods, idols, and sin alongside of the God whom we claim as Lord! Whose name are we really walking in then? We are just like the people in Micah 4:5. Our actions don't line up with our words. We go to the Lord's house to be taught how to walk in His ways, and then we walk in the ways of our flesh the very moment we leave God's house and His teaching.

We tend to let every continuous sin off the hook, knowing it is sin and that it is displeasing to God. We choose to keep them alive. We do not crucify them. We just keep letting them off the hook by setting them aside to presumably deal with later. We constantly refuse to see our need to be rid of them. We think that God either winks at them or just turns His holy eyes away from them. We simply do not care at all that we have been called to a walk of holiness. These are the telltale signs that we are "sparing" our gods, our idols, and our sin instead of taking full vengeance on them. This is true spiritual complacency.

Look again at the definition of the word "sparing," but this time look at it in light of your own gods. Do you recognize your own disobedience? Choose the most prevalent sin in your life and put its name in for the word "god" below:

1. Reviving my god—by bringing it back to life again and again after Jesus has killed it.

2. Keeping, leaving, or making my god alive (a new sin)—by willingly giving it life.

3. Nourishing my god—by feeding it to keep it alive and refusing to starve it.

4. Preserving my god—by doing what it takes to keep it alive and active in my life.

5. Repairing or restoring my god—by making adjustments in order to keep it alive and active, like it used to be.

Can you see where you are disobeying God's call to take full vengeance on your gods? Did the light bulb just go on? By sparing the women, Israel left the door wide open to be influenced again by false gods. When we let our sins be spared, we open a door to the enemy to gain victory again and again in our lives. When we walk in our sins, according to the flesh, our level of holiness is directly affected. In actuality, our gods reveal just how un-Christlike we truly are. Sometimes we can take some ground back from the enemy who seeks to lure us away from God, but if we don't wipe out the entire stronghold, then we are just continuing to allow our sins to co-exist with the Spirit within us. We must learn how to bring our sins to a complete death. Then your responsibility will be to pay close attention to those areas where you have gained victory by continuing to keep that sin out of your heart. That is how you can stand firm in not reviving or restoring your former gods.

OUR COMPLACENT HEARTS

Let's take it all the way back to the beginning. Israel's downfall was not in the keeping of women and booty. Their downfall was the moment that they disobeyed the words of God spoken through Moses. God's commands meant very little, if anything, to them once the temptation was before their eyes. We disobey in the exact same way, by the same process. Can you relate to these statements?

1. We like what we see, we want it, and we grab it.

2. We like what gratifies our flesh, even when God has clearly said, "No!"

3. We want to be in control and not be told by God or anyone else what to do or not to do.

4. We want to please ourselves more than we want to please God.

5. We lack the desire to be in a relationship with God that will require our obedience.

When I was teaching this material in my small group, one quiet, but thoughtful, man added one more thing to this list. This was his comment.

6. We think that we are bullet-proof and invisible.

I like that answer. I find it to be completely true! We tend to think that we can sin and get away with it because God surely wouldn't discipline us harshly, would He? Or we think that He is paying very poor attention to His children, and we might be able to slip one more sin by Him.

Maybe these illustrations don't fit you. Maybe they do not describe the truth about why you disobey your Lord. If not, please take some time to identify why you do not obey God's commands, or only partially obey them. Understanding why we continue to disobey is an important part of the process of learning to obey.

Think back now to the Tabernacle. Do you remember the courts and their purposes? If you have been hanging around in the Outer Court, comfortable enough in your salvation and baptism, oblivious to the victory over sin that God is calling you to, it is time for you to take a step into the Inner Court of obedience. Are you already in the Inner Court, enjoying the Holy Spirit's company and the Word, but still living in cyclical sin? Then it's time for you to put shoe leather on the soles of your spiritual walking shoes! It's time to take some serious vengeance on your sin! Are you willing now for your heart to be laid bare before you and the Lord so that the idols and sin can be removed? If you are not willing, you will not be able to grow any closer to God than you currently are. Are you satisfied with that, and satisfied with living your small "g" god-driven life?

God sent Israel to war! This will be no less a battle for us, and it will likely last for our entire life. Will God find you obedient to this call, or will you take the easiest, most flesh-pleasing way out? The first will lead you to victory and intimacy with God; the other will eventually defeat you and keep you from drawing near to God. The choice, ultimately, is yours. Choose wisely. Choose to take full vengeance on your sin. The alternative is only foolishness, and ultimately it reveals your complacency. Consider these wise words that speak of this kind of complacency.

> Complacency is a blight that saps energy, dulls attitudes, and causes a drain on the brain. The first symptom is satisfaction with things as they are. The second is rejection of things as they might be. "Good enough" becomes today's watchword and tomorrow's standard. Complacency makes people fear the unknown, mistrust the untried, and abhor the new. Like water, complacent people follow the easiest course—downhill. They draw false strength from looking back.[1]

INTROSPECTION

1. When we don't take full vengeance on our gods and sin, we actually create the circumstances that will allow them to grow up in us. Are you nourishing your weeds, or are you pulling them up and destroying them?

2. What influence do your gods and sin have on your spiritual growth?

3. God wanted the Israelites to eradicate all foreign gods from their lives by taking *full vengeance* on them. What does God want you to do with your identified gods and sin?

4. There were severe consequences for Israel when they disobeyed God and kept the foreign gods alive by sparing (giving life to) the women of idolatry. Are you willing to find out what God's consequences will be for you if you choose to let your gods and sin live, instead of destroying them? Do you think that you are "bullet-proof"?

5. Why does God discipline us when we disobey? How do your gods and sin affect your holiness?

ENDNOTE

1. *Bits & Pieces* (May 28, 1992), 15, www.sermonillustrations.com/a-z/c/complacency.htm.

CHAPTER 8

FULLY FOLLOWING GOD'S COMMANDS

Though you were slaves of sin, you became obedient from the heart... (Romans 6:17).

Elisabeth Elliot, at Urbana 76, told of her brother Thomas Howard. Their mother let him play with paper bags she'd saved if he put them away afterwards. One day she walked into the kitchen to find them strewn all over the floor. Tom was out at the piano with his father singing hymns. When confronted, he protested, "But Mom, I want to sing." His father stated, "It's no good singing God's praise if you're disobedient."[1]

At the end of the last chapter, I asked you to consider a few questions, the last being this: What are you willing to commit to in your battle over your gods in order to gain victory over them and their rule in your life? As believers in the Lord Jesus Christ, we should desire to make Him the only God in our lives, yet we struggle with just how to get that done. Our hearts are filled with many sins and "gods," as we saw in Chapter 6, and we know that we are commanded to take full vengeance on them. When we look at the work ahead of us, we see that we are merely at the beginning of what could be a very long process of clearing out what keeps us from the intimacy with God that we long for and know is available to us. In Matthew 26:41, Jesus said, *"The spirit is willing, but the flesh is weak."* If we are truly honest with ourselves, we likely want to opt out of taking full vengeance on the gods in our hearts. The result of such a choice will be that our sin will produce thick roots that will be much more difficult to cut out later. Why do we so often make this poor choice? At the heart of the matter is the fact that we really do not want to obey God's call to dispossess them from our hearts.

BREAKING GOD'S HEART

Our willful disobedience as born-again children of the Living God breaks the heart of the Father who loves us so much, of Jesus who left His home in Heaven and died in our place, and of the Spirit who longs to sanctify and complete us. It also brings into our lives the consequences of it, the fruit of disobedience. Have you been there? Has your walk ever faltered and felt empty because you are walking in a known sin rather than in the Spirit? Have you felt the discipline of Daddy for breaking His commands? Or maybe you have just simply been walking your own journey, disregarding the instruction and illumination that the Spirit can give. Disobedience has many faces, but none of them is God's reflection in us. Ultimately, when we disobey on a regular basis, our holiness and Christlikeness is threatened. We begin to lose the ground that we have gained in the past, and our reflection looks like the face of the world, instead of the face of God.

God does not want us to let our sin off the hook! And He is not nearly as interested in our, "I'm sorry," as He is in our confession of sin and repentance. Have you ever heard children (and sometimes adults!) say that they are sorry when they really are just sorry that they got caught and are now in trouble? It goes a little something like this: "Mary, tell your brother that you are sorry for taking his train engine away from him." Several moments pass, so you prompt, "Mary. . ." With all the iciness and attitude of a snow queen, you hear this come from your precious little girl, "Sorr-rreeee!" Moments later, little brother is screaming again for his train engine. Get the picture?

There is a huge difference between telling God that you are sorry for something that you have done and a true confession with a repentant heart. Saying, "Sorry, God," becomes our quick way to get back into His good graces, or at least that is what we tend to think. If we feel that response hasn't gotten us very far with God, we will usually put a "Please forgive me" with it. Don't get me wrong. Telling God that you are sorry and asking for His forgiveness is not wrong at all. As a matter of fact, we should tell God we are sorry and thank Him for forgiving us. But if that is as far as we go, then our response is not a confession to God at all. A confession to God is agreeing with God on these two things—that you know that you are wrong because you are seeing your sin from His perspective and that you do not want to repeat the offense. God wants our confession to lead to something other than the repeated performance of, "I'm sorry, please forgive me." He desires that our truly contrite confession will lead to our future obedience.

Obedience to our Holy God is critical on our journey toward a heart that is no longer divided by its wrong priorities, sin, and idols. Our obedience is the one thing that sets us apart from the world in how we handle life's situations and choices. Obedience is the ongoing, outward sign of an inner transformation. In this chapter, we are going to visit another two chapters of the Old Testament in order to see how important fully following God's every command is to us and Him. We will also look at a more familiar passage in the New Testament to see how we can take our stand against an enemy whose goal it is to lead us into all forms of disobedience, trap us in our sin, and keep us in bondage to it.

GOD'S RESPONSE TO DISOBEDIENCE

Our lesson is found in Numbers 32:1-10. After you read it here, we will look at three powerful points that must sink down deeply into our spirits so that we can know how we are to "take full vengeance on our sin by fully following God's commands."

> *Now the sons of Reuben and the sons of Gad had an exceedingly large number of livestock. So when they saw the land of Jazer and the land of Gilead, that it was indeed a place suitable for livestock, the sons of Gad and the sons of Reuben came and spoke to Moses and to Eleazar the priest and to the leaders of the congregation, saying, "Ataroth, Dibon, Jazer, Nimrah, Heshbon, Elealeh, Sebam, Nebo and Beon, the land which the Lord conquered*

before the congregation of Israel, is a land for livestock, and your servants have livestock." They said, "If we have found favor in your sight, let this land be given to your servants as a possession; do not take us across the Jordan." But Moses said to the sons of Gad and to the sons of Reuben, "Shall your brothers go to war while you yourselves sit here? Now why are you discouraging the sons of Israel from crossing over into the land which the Lord has given them? This is what your fathers did when I sent them from Kadesh-barnea to see the land. For when they went up to the valley of Eshcol and saw the land, they discouraged the sons of Israel so that they did not go into the land which the Lord had given them. So the Lord's anger burned in that day, and He swore, saying, 'None of the men who came up from Egypt, from twenty years old and upward, shall see the land which I swore to Abraham, to Isaac and to Jacob; for they did not follow Me fully, except Caleb the son of Jephunneh the Kenizzite and Joshua the son of Nun, for they have followed the Lord fully.' So the Lord's anger burned against Israel, and He made them wander in the wilderness forty years, until the entire generation of those who had done evil in the sight of the Lord was destroyed. Now behold, you have risen up in your fathers' place, a brood of sinful men, to add still more to the burning anger of the Lord against Israel. For if you turn away from following Him, He will once more abandon them in the wilderness, and you will destroy all these people."

Moses is recounting the story of God sending out the 12 spies, one from each of the 12 tribes of Israel, to look at the land that the Israelites would possess following their exodus from Egypt. Ten of the spies saw that the land was "flowing with milk and honey," but they were afraid of the people who already lived there—the people they would now have to dispossess (remove) from the land. They came back and discouraged their clans, causing them to also fear going into the land. But Joshua and Caleb, the other two spies, followed the Lord's command to the letter. They returned and tried to encourage the people that the Lord would be faithful in all He had commanded them to do. They were the only spies who completely followed the command of God. Here is our first point to consider:

Point #1: God wants our complete and full compliance to His words and commands.

Look back at the text. God said this about His people, including the ten spies, who came up out of bondage in Egypt: *"They did not follow Me fully."* But about Joshua and Caleb, the two faithful spies He said, "They followed Me fully."

Did you notice that God did not praise the ten spies for the time they spent spying in the Promised Land for His people? He did not praise them for their bravery and courage as they witnessed giants in the land. He also did not praise them for the gigantic clusters of grapes they brought back from the land or for the pomegranates or figs they found. Have you ever wondered why it mattered to God to what degree they followed Him and His commands? You have to understand what God's purpose and goal was for His chosen people. It was to give them the Promised Land to live and dwell in. His goal was to lead His obedient children out of the wilderness that they had been traveling through and lead them into the beautiful and lush land of promise.

OUR SPIRITUAL WALK COMPARED TO ISRAEL'S JOURNEY

Now, let's make Point #1 relevant to us. Consider this concept that I want to share with you. This is another picture of the journey to the complete healing of your broken spiritual heart. It is very similar to the picture of the Tabernacle that we viewed in Chapters 1 through 4.

You hopefully have walked through the door of the Tabernacle into your salvation. If you have, then at the same time you have walked out of your Egypt, the place of your spiritual bondage. Now you are set free from the penalty of your sin, but you may have not yet arrived at your Promised Land, the daily presence of the Living God. You have entered into the Outer Court where you have reveled in your salvation and followed God, but you have not constantly been obedient. You, in a sense, are wandering there in a wilderness, not quite understanding how to consistently obey.

Then, when you purposefully stepped into the Inner Court (if you have), you found it to be a place where you began to remove (dispossess) the gods and sins that were in your "land"—your hearts. This can be likened to the "crossing of the Jordan into the Promised Land," where the Israelites began to remove the inhabitants because they were idolaters that worshiped other gods. Sanctification takes place in you, in the Inner Courts where you begin to experience the Promised Land by systematically removing all that is in opposition to the God of your heart. A similar cleansing of idol worship took place in Canaan, the Israelite's Promised Land, before they would be allowed to live there.

Once all of the people and their false gods were removed, then Israel could live daily in the constant and abiding presence of their God, in His blessing and favor. This is why it is the Land of the Promise. If Israel would do everything that God commanded them, by removing all who were in opposition to Him, they would live in paradise on earth.

That was God's plan—for His children to live in the land and worship only Him. The same is true for you. Your Promised Land, having had all of your false gods removed, will be like living intimately with your God—in the Holy of Holies—alone, with no other gods but the one true God. Do you see that? Do you understand how you fit into the picture God gave us from the journey of the Israelites? We are to journey from our bondage all the way to the presence of the Living God! The goal of the Tabernacle is to reach the Holy of Holies, to have been made holy and like Christ, to be living maturely by the purity of our hearts. The goal of the Israelites, set free from their bondage in Egypt, was to live in the Promised Land, a land with its idols removed. The Promised Land was a picture of God in the center of the lives of His chosen ones who walked in unity with Him and Him alone. It is a picture, as well, of the godly, sin-healed heart of a Christian!

But most of us are still either in the Outer Court of our salvation or the Inner Court of our sanctification. Either way, we are being prepared to enter into the Holy of Holies, our Promised Land, the land of our truest intimacy with our God. And if we want to step through the veil into the most intimate place with God, we must clearly understand the next point.

Our Armor and Plan

Point #2: We must be fully armed when we cross into that place in our journey to the "Promised Land" of the Holy of Holies where our gods will be dispossessed. We must be prepared for this battle, and we must know what God's battle plan is.

Had Israel crossed the Jordan without any weapons, they would have most surely been annihilated. The people who had been living there would certainly have banded together against an unarmed foe, and the defeat would have been a crushing blow to God's chosen people. Without a battle plan, there would have been no organization, and therefore, no victory for God's people. The same is going to be true for us if we attempt to just "go in" and destroy every god, idol, attitude, or sin in our hearts that is contrary to God and His purposes. Without weapons and a battle plan, we will fall to an enemy who does not want his territory encroached upon!

God has given us the perfect plan of attack when it comes to our spiritual battles, and the armor and weapons that He has chosen for us are perfect as well. As our Commander-in-Chief, He has set us up to be victorious, if we will but utilize what He has already given us. The problem is that we seldom choose to enter into this kind of battle, and when we do, our armor seems cumbersome to us because we have not been trained for this kind of war. We are usually unarmed and unprepared because we have not even attended spiritual "boot camp," so we are ill-equipped for the battle with the forces of darkness.

God has given us an armor that we are to wear when dispossessing sin from our hearts. It is made up of individual pieces that are intended to be used by us to gain victory over our sin and our enemy. Paul eloquently describes it for us:

> *Finally, be strong in the Lord and in the strength of His might. Put on the full armor of God, so that you will be able to stand firm against the schemes of the devil. For our struggle is not against flesh and blood, but against the rulers, against the powers, against the world forces of the darkness, against*

*the spiritual forces of wickedness in the heavenly places. Therefore, take up
the full armor of God, so that you will be able to resist in the evil day, and
having done everything, to stand firm. Stand firm therefore, having girded
your loins with the [belt of] truth, and having put on the breastplate of
righteousness, and having shod your feet with the preparation of the gospel
of peace; in addition to all, taking up the shield of faith with which you
will be able to extinguish all the flaming arrows of the evil one. And take
the helmet of salvation, and the sword of the Spirit, which is the word of
God. With all prayer and petition pray at all times in the Spirit, and with
this in view, be on the alert with perseverance and petition for all the saints*
(Ephesians 6:10-18).

We are specifically told to put on the full armor, not just a piece of
it. We are not to try to use only part of it at a time when it comes to doing battle. It is designed to be used as one whole unit. It was meant to be
taken into battle in full! Isn't it interesting that God has told us to take
full vengeance on those things that keep us from becoming Christlike? He
has told us to fully follow His commands. And now He says to us to put
on and use the full armor that He has prepared for us. God doesn't want
anything done partially!

Taking this passage now verse by verse, let's see just how powerful
this armor can be. When we set out to dispossess something evil in our
hearts, we will definitely need the strength of God to do that. However,
God isn't just going to step in, put on our armor Himself, and charge at
our enemy. Instead, we are called to do that. In wearing and implementing
the armor, God's strength becomes ours. We need not muster our own
strength, but instead, move forward in His! Using this armor will bring to
us the strength of God to overcome any attack of the enemy.

We are to put on all of this armor in order that we will be able to stand
firm against satan's schemes. What schemes might the enemy use against
us? We don't have to get specific to know that he is all about stealing from
us, killing us, and destroying us (see John 10:10). But he only has one
weapon—lies! If he can get us to believe his lies, then he has control over
us in that area. Often, if we are not careful, we end up in spiritual bondage
to the enemy. But if we use our armor against the lies, then they won't be

able to penetrate the armor and injure our hearts in the journey. And since all of our battles are spiritual in nature, this spiritual armor is going to have the greatest impact and effect on satan and his forces of evil. This armor is to be used to resist any ploy that satan might fling at us. If used properly, we will find ourselves standing firm as the enemy retreats until a more opportune time, when he hopes that we will be less prepared for battle.

THE BELT OF TRUTH

Now let's analyze the armor of warfare, piece by piece, and learn what can be accomplished by each. Paul, the author of the letter to the Ephesians, begins with the belt of truth. Why would the Spirit lead him to start there? I doubt we can know for sure, but I do know this: nothing is written in the Word without His touch. So, I will offer just one suggestion. Do you recall what satan's only weapon is? It is his lies. There is only one thing that I know of, for sure, that has the power to overcome a lie—the truth! Our ability to know and grasp the truth is of great value to us in this fight! When we begin to refuse to believe the lies anymore, victory is just around the corner. No matter how strong a Christian you are, satan's lies have infiltrated your heart, your mind, and possibly even your actions. But the battle always begins with a thought in your mind. Battles, more often than not, begin with a lie.

Do you pay close attention to your thoughts? I have begun to for this very reason. I know that when I want to say something to myself, I phrase it somewhat like this: "Now, why didn't I think to stop and pick up milk on the way home?" But there are times when in the same situation I hear it more like this: "You are so dumb. It's just like you to forget. You always forget." Do you see the difference? I don't talk to myself with the second person pronoun "you." I talk to myself with the first person pronouns "I" and "me." Second person pronouns are used when someone is talking to you. This is an important point. Who is talking to me, if I'm not the one talking? It can either be the Spirit or the enemy. But it is the enemy for sure if your thoughts are in the second person (you!) and have an accusatory tone. He accuses the saints. The Holy Spirit never does.

The Spirit's words might sound more like this, "You have been very distracted today. Fix your eyes on Me when you are distracted. I will help you remember, if you will." The Spirit convicts; the enemy accuses and whispers his lies to us every chance he gets. Remember, his lies are his only weapon, so it is critical that we learn to combat them with the truth.

So, just how do you handle this in battle mode when it happens? The best way that I know is to speak the truth out loud to satan immediately. Speaking out loud is important, because satan is not all-knowing. He cannot read our thoughts. Saying something along these lines seems to work: "It is not dumb of me to forget to stop and get milk. I have been preoccupied thinking about _____. And by the way, I rarely forget. This is not my usual habit!"

I know that this example is very simplistic, and many of you have experienced the lies of the enemy regarding some very deep and hurtful things from your past. This is still practical and useful to you, though you may have to work very hard to identify the false belief system and its associated lies. Once identified and accepted as a lie, you still have to replace the false thought with truth. A Christian counselor, your pastor, or a close Christian friend might be beneficial, as they might be helpful in pointing out thoughts that are lies. And of course, the Word of God is your best source! No matter to what degree you experience false beliefs, fighting the lies with truth is always your best answer. We are to strap on the belt of truth in order to overcome the lies that the enemy will always tell us.

THE BREASTPLATE OF RIGHTEOUSNESS

The next piece of armor spoken of is the breastplate of righteousness. This piece of the armor is critical if we are going to protect our "hearts." The breastplate was a shield that covered the major organs of the body. Spiritually speaking, it covers our heart. If we are going to fully follow God's commands by taking full vengeance on our sins so that we can have a heart that is united and healed by God, then we must use this breastplate in the battle. Christ's righteousness was credited to us at the point of our salvation. We were justified in the eyes of our Lord. In other words, in God's eyes, it was "just as if" we had never sinned. But there is another righteousness that we must focus on now that we are saved. It is the righteousness of holy living. In order to live a holy lifestyle, and thus live righteously, we must use the breastplate that protects us from this kind of warfare, making right choices in the midst of the battle of temptation.

Too often we think about making the right choices after we have been tempted and fall prey to the enemy's scheme by making a wrong and sinful choice. That is why the breastplate of righteousness should be practiced and exercised every day so that at the moment of great temptation, it will be second nature to us to make the right choice. You must practice seeing yourself as Christ sees you—righteous—and do what a righteous one would do.

PEACEFUL FEET

Moving down to the very bottom of our armor, Paul introduces to us the shoes prepared with the Gospel of peace. As Jesus was going through His final teachings to the disciples, He told them this:

Peace I leave with you, My peace I give to you; not as the world gives do I give you. Do not let your heart be troubled, nor let it be fearful (John 14:27).

All that Jesus spoke to His disciples in John 13–17 was critical information if they were to be successful in carrying the Gospel to the world in His physical absence. He knew that His peace would be necessary for their victory over an enemy that would stop at nothing to destroy them and the Gospel. Jesus' Gospel was one of peace with God. He was telling His disciples of their need to settle the issue now. They were never again to doubt their position with God, and never fear that again. Jesus was calling them to be assured of their salvation and to walk in it.

Isn't it interesting that God used the word picture of a sandal or shoe to illustrate how we are to "walk out" the Gospel? Because we are God's children, our journey is to be traveled with our shoes of peace and assurance tightly tied on. Our peace with God that flows out of our understanding of God's love for us is something that must be settled in our hearts before we try to overcome our daily sin. Walking in the knowledge of His love for us is what our peace is based upon, and it is critical to our belief system. Without this peace in our hearts, it will be difficult to overcome the lies the enemy will tell us, especially when we fail by falling to sin. Without the peace of knowing that God loves us, even when we fail Him, we might just believe the lie of satan that it is impossible to belong to God if we sin.

Also critical to our walk of peace is the manner in which we walk through our terrifying times of the journey. When Jesus said, *"Do not let your heart be troubled, nor let it be fearful,"* He was just hours away from His arrest, trial, crucifixion, and death. He knew that His disciples would face a time of despair and heartache. He knew that in their flesh they would be fearful of what would come next. But isn't it amazing that He also left these words for us, knowing that we, too, would face our own dark days? His peace was the answer then, and it is still the answer for us today. Jesus is calling each of us today to walk out our spiritual battles by standing firm in the peace that has been given to us by God.

THE SHIELD OF FAITH

In order to have that kind of peace, we have to believe that in all situations God is in control. No matter what our circumstances are, no matter what method of attack the enemy uses against us, and no matter what sin we are trying to rid from our lives, we must have the faith that God knows our situation and will be in control of it, if we will release our control. This is the shield of faith that is spoken of as part of the spiritual armor we are to wear. It is our faith in God in the midst of every facet of our lives that helps us to extinguish the arrows that satan will inevitably shoot at each one of us.

THE HELMET AND THE SWORD

So that our minds will be protected, we are called to take the helmet of salvation and the sword of the Spirit. Their use together is critical. It is necessary that we see the connection between the two. To me, to use them together is to join the two major parts of the life of every Christian—our salvation and our sanctification. To put on the helmet of salvation is to protect the mind from lies by standing on the truth of our adoption into

God's family by the forgiveness He offers us. But we are also supposed to wield the sword of the Spirit, the very Word of God, against the enemy and his lies. It is by the Word itself that our minds become transformed. Then we can begin to walk in the Spirit, instead of conforming to the world and its ways. Overcoming sin in our life is the result of our constant study of the Word and our surrender of those sinful parts of our lives to the rule of the Holy Spirit within us.

PRAYERS AND PETITIONS

Last, but certainly not least, are our prayers and petitions at all times—times of success, failure, ease, and attack. By praying ahead of time, we are more alert to the attacks the enemy will bring against us. By praying, we are able to put all the rest of the armor to work for our victory over the sin in our lives. Do you see how interconnected the armor and constant prayer are? Prayers and petitions are the oil in the oil can that the rusted Tin Man so desperately needed to move effectively in his "body armor." Without the oil, he was destined to be immoveable forever!

With no desire to drive out the gods in our lives, we stand no chance of overcoming them. When we have no desire to drive out the evil in us, we tend to walk in evil, leaving the sin in our hearts for the enemy to use against us over and over. If we want to win spiritual victories, we must make the conscious decision to apply (put on) and implement (use) the armor of which Paul speaks. It's not a gift that we receive that works all by itself! The full armor of God becomes a useless weapon to us when we allow our gods to keep us from fully following after God and all of His ways. The laziness of our walk not only renders the armor useless, but it also renders the armor-bearing soldier useless as well.

YOU CAN'T HIDE FOREVER

Remembering Points #1 and #2, that God wants our complete and full compliance to His words and commands and that we must be fully armed in order to dispossess the gods of our hearts, let's move on to the last point.

Point #3: Your sin will find you out eventually.

Return now to Numbers 32. It is there that we will see our third point made with several exclamation points! In this chapter, Israel was preparing to cross the Jordan River into the Promised Land. But the tribes of Reuben and Gad and the half-tribe of Manasseh wanted to make their home on the east side of the Jordan. These tribes were compared to the ten spies who saw the fruitfulness of the land when Israel came out of bondage but were afraid of the people and the fortified cities found there. These two and a half tribes were not seen as being like Joshua and Caleb, the two spies who trusted God and tried to convince all of Israel that they should "take possession of the land and overcome it." Instead, they were seen as men who were shirking their God-given responsibilities to take full vengeance on the people of the Promised Land and completely dispossess them. They appear to be trying to dodge the bullet, no pun intended!

By the wise counsel of Moses, their leader, and Eleazar, their priest, these men and their families were given permission to remain on the east side of the Jordan, but not before they fulfilled the commandment of God with their fellow tribesmen. They would first have to help their brothers drive out the inhabitants of the Promised Land before settling their families east of the Jordan. When all the people were dispossessed, only then could the tribes cross back over to the east side of the Jordan and live there.

Here is the place in the story where we see our third point clearly. Look at verses 20-24 below to see exactly what Moses said to them:

> ...If you will do this, if you will arm yourselves before the Lord for the war, and all of you armed men cross over the Jordan before the Lord until He has driven His enemies out from before Him, and the land is subdued before the Lord, then afterward you shall return and be free of obligation toward the Lord and toward Israel, and this land shall be yours for a possession before the Lord. But if you will not do so, behold, you have sinned against the Lord, and be sure your sin will find you out. Build yourselves cities for your little ones, and sheepfolds for your sheep, and do what you have promised (Numbers 32:20-24).

My children always hated it when I told them the manner in which I would often pray about them. They knew that their father and I could not possibly be aware of every little thing they did. I knew that, too! So I prayed frequently that God would always show me the things that were being kept hidden from me. Many times I became aware of what I could not have possibly known on my own.

God knows everything, like I wanted to know with my children. However, He doesn't need to have anything revealed to Him. And He won't allow the sins in our hearts to go on forever. Eventually, they will find us out. From experience, I know that it is far better for me to deal with them as God brings them to my mind than to have them find me out in severe and embarrassing situations.

DREADFUL CONSEQUENCES

So what are the results of not driving out the inhabitants (sins) of your heart, when you willfully disobey God's command to remove them? Two verses in the following chapter show us what the result of our disobedience will be. Let me warn you…you probably won't like what you find here any more than I did! God spoke these words to Israel as He directed them to remove everyone from the land He had promised them. He could not have been more clear and exact. His words are prophetic, for this is just what happened to Israel.

> *But if you do not drive out the inhabitants of the land from before you, then it shall come about that those whom you let remain of them will become as pricks in your eyes and as thorns in your sides, and they will trouble you in the land in which you live. And as I plan to do to them, so I will do to you* (Numbers 33:55-56).

When we let our sin off of God's hook and ours, this is the result:

1. Your sins will become as pricks in your eyes.

2. Your sins will become as thorns in your side.

3. Your sins will cause you continual trouble.

4. Your sins might cause your very destruction.

Do you see that the sin that you allow to remain in your heart, possessing God's home in you, will become the very snare that traps you in its bondage? Our full obedience to God's commands, to His call to holiness, is critical when it comes to dispossessing our sins and gods. Our full obedience is critical to our spiritual life and growth. God takes very seriously our following Him fully, as you can see by these stories recorded for our instruction. When it comes to our gods and our sin, what God intends to see destroyed in us can actually end up destroying us! As always, it is our choice as to whether we will fully follow God's commands to take full vengeance on our sin or willfully disobey Him and ignore them. It seems beyond ridiculous that we would choose any other way.

Neil Marten, a member of the British Parliament, was once giving a group of his constituents a guided tour of the Houses of Parliament. During the course of the visit, the group happened to meet Lord Hailsham, then Lord Chancellor, wearing all the regalia of his office. Hailsham recognized Marten among the group and cried, "Neil!" Not daring to question or disobey the "command," the entire band of visitors promptly fell to their knees![2]

Can God say that you are taking such a proactive approach to obeying His command to take full vengeance on your sins and idols?

Take a moment and think about what sin you want to overcome on purpose, by fully focusing on its dispossession from your heart for good. It is time for the gods that want to keep you trapped in bondage to sin to be removed! Begin with appropriating the armor every day, working on just one idol or sin. Do this for one week. God wants your full compliance to His command to be holy because He is. He has given you the perfect armor with which to protect yourself from that sin, and to stand strong in Him. And remember, your sin will always find you out. Take it on today! Defeat it with the transforming of your mind by renewing it in the truth of the Word! Your sword, the very Word of God, is a dangerous weapon intended to be used on the father of lies! Use it to push them out of your heart and mind.

Thomas à Kempis once said, "Instant obedience is the only kind of obedience there is; delayed obedience is disobedience. Whoever strives to withdraw from obedience, withdraws from grace."[3]

Walk in obedience to His commands by doing what you are supposed to do, for this is God's plan for you!

INTROSPECTION

1. What have the results of your willful disobedience been?

2. What is the difference between telling God we are sorry for our sin and confessing our sin to Him or another person? Which one is more sincere? Why?

3. How did the response of the Israelites and ten of the spies (when they learned about the giants in the land) differ from Joshua and Caleb's response?

4. Why does our full compliance with God's commands make a difference to Him?

5. How can you better use the full armor of God to dispossess the gods in your heart? Will you?

ENDNOTES

1. Elisabeth Elliot, www.sermonillustrations.com/a-z/d/disobedience.htm.

2. *Today in the Word* (July 30, 1993), www.sermonillustrations.com/a-z/o/obedience.htm.

3. Thomas à Kempis, www.sermonillustrations.com/a-z/o/obedience.htm.

SECTION THREE

OUR SURRENDER

CHAPTER 9

SURRENDERING TO THE PROCESS

Therefore I urge you, brethren, by the mercies of God, to present your bodies a living and holy sacrifice, acceptable to God, which is your spiritual service of worship (Romans 12:1).

The captain of the ship looked into the dark night and saw faint lights in the distance. Immediately he told his signalman to send a message: "Alter your course 10 degrees south." Promptly a return message was received: "Alter your course 10 degrees north." The captain was angered; his command had been ignored. So he sent a second message: "Alter your course 10 degrees south—I am the captain!" Soon another message was received: "Alter your course 10 degrees north—I am seaman third class Jones." Immediately the captain sent a third message, knowing the fear it would evoke: "Alter your course 10 degrees south—I am a battleship." Then the reply came. "Alter your course 10 degrees north—I am a lighthouse."

In the midst of our dark and foggy times, all sorts of voices are shouting orders into the night, telling us what to do, how to adjust our lives. Out of the darkness, one voice signals something quite opposite to the rest—something almost absurd. But the voice happens to be the Light of the World, and we ignore it at our peril.[1]

Surrendering to the voice of God is the call of and command to every believer, and it is vital to the process of spiritual growth. But we all seem to have trouble bending to the higher authority. We so desperately want to remain in control of our lives, struggling with the concept of surrendering and submission to anyone, let alone God. We much prefer, with booming voice, to tell God what we will and won't do, often expecting Him to be the one to alter His course for us.

In this last section of *Spiritual Healing*, we are going to consider this call to surrender, learn of the power that is available when we surrender to God, what it will take to endure, and how to walk obediently by the Spirit. But first, we must examine the meaning of the word *"surrender"*.

SURRENDER DEFINED

It's time to tie up all that we have learned so far with a pretty bow. Hopefully this will help you see the bigger picture of all that the Spirit has been trying to teach us. We are on a journey toward the face of God, toward the greatest intimacy with Him that we can experience in this life. This journey has included the study of the Tabernacle and how it applies to our walk of faith. It has included an in-depth look into our own hearts filled with sin and idols, and what God wants us to do with the idols we found there. The bow that ties it all together can be summed up in just one word— *"surrender"*. Oswald Chambers said it like this: "There is only one thing God wants of us, and that is our unconditional surrender."[2]

What words or pictures come to your mind when you hear or think of the word *"surrender"*? A lost battle? Giving up? Throwing in the towel? Do you consider it a negative thing? Let's take a look at what *Webster's New World Dictionary* has to say about surrender. Here is how it is defined as a transitive verb: "1. To give up possession of or power over; yield to another on demand or compulsion 2. to give up claim to; give over or yield, esp. voluntarily, as in favor of another 3. to give up or abandon 4. to yield or resign (oneself) to an emotion, influence, etc." and as an intransitive verb: "I. to give oneself up to another's power or control, esp. as a prisoner 2. to give in (to something); yield."[3]

Generally, the word *"surrender"* means to give up something completely, after striving to maintain possession of it. Are you making the spiritual connection? Our flesh keeps trying to hang onto the control of our lives, and that control can be seen every time that we fall prey to temptation. The sin that follows the temptation is a clear indication that we are controlled in that area by our flesh. Isaiah spoke about our flesh, spelling out the truth about it:

> *All flesh is grass, and all its loveliness is like the flower of the field. The grass withers, the flower fades, when the breath of the Lord blows upon it; surely the people are grass. The grass withers, the flower fades, but the word of our God stands forever* (Isaiah 40:6b-8).

Isaiah compares people who are fleshly with grass and flowers. According to the verses, our flesh is in a constant state of decline! Not only are we withering and fading physically, but our sinful flesh also desires to take over our whole lives. Our flesh wants to be in control and make all the decisions based on what will please and feed it. When our flesh is in control, a spiritual death begins to take place. While we might be spiritually growing and our walk improving, our flesh continues to get worse and worse. Flesh never improves. It has no ability to improve. It is always in the state of withering and declining. The older you get, the more clearly you can see this truth in action. You need to look no further than Paul's lament in Romans 7. Paul, the transformed apostle of the Lord Jesus Christ who was responsible for so many of the epistles that teach us today, soundly judged his own flesh (and ours as well) when he said this:

> *For I know that nothing good dwells in me, that is, in my flesh; for the willing is present in me, but the doing of the good is not* (Romans 7:18).

When we continue to follow our flesh, we allow its sinful and selfish ways to maintain control of our lives. We become the god of our lives when we allow our own flesh to sit on the throne upon which the Spirit is to be sitting. When we are the god of our own life, we continue doing what we want to do. In this state, we are unwilling to yield to the very God we clung to for our salvation.

POINTS OF SURRENDER

Can you recall the picture of the Tabernacle in your mind? Look back at it, if you can't. Where was the point of our first surrender? Wasn't it at the door when we stepped into a relationship with God through Jesus? It was when we were saved that we first surrendered ourselves to God. Salvation is surrender.

Where was the next point of surrender? Very likely it was when we followed the command of Christ to be baptized, thus identifying ourselves with Christ. Baptism is surrender.

Where else has surrender been required of us? If you have entered into the Inner Court, many forms of surrender have been necessary for you to begin walking in the Spirit, spending time daily in the Word, and learning how to truly worship our Lord. Our truest form of surrender in the Inner Court will come when we consistently walk in obedience to God's commands and will. Obedience is surrender.

Finally, there was a required surrender in order to enter through the veil into the Holy of Holies. It was more demanding than all of the other forms of surrender. It was the surrender of our whole life, the crucifixion of our flesh. In this surrender, God becomes our total focus. It is abandonment to God. This reckless abandonment to God is the ultimate form of surrender.

Just as our walk of faith has been a progression, we must be able to understand as well that our surrender to the God of our lives is also progressively achieved. Let's look back again at a verse we have already investigated. Let these words of Isaiah settle a little more deeply into your heart:

A highway will be there, a roadway, and it will be called the Highway of Holiness. The unclean will not travel on it, but it will be for him who walks that way, and fools will not wander on it (Isaiah 35:8).

Compare that now with Luke 3:4b-5 and see what it says to us:

Make ready the way of the Lord, make His paths straight. Every ravine will be filled, and every mountain and hill will be brought low; the crooked will become straight, and the rough roads smooth.

From what we have learned in the previous chapters, we can sum up and applicably live out these two verses by:

- Bringing to God the mountain of sins that have been found in our hearts.

- Giving Him full authority and control over them.

- Joining the work of God by taking full vengeance on them.

- Seeking to obey God's every command.

This is true surrender. This is the way to put ourselves on the Highway of Holiness, and it should be the intentional walk of every believer who wishes to walk in the Spirit by surrender and obedience. There is only one way to make the rough roadways of our heart smooth—God's way, the highway of holiness, the road of surrender. When we don't choose to surrender fully to the Lord, we wear the name "fool." And a fool will continue on his own pathway, doing whatever he pleases. But God's way is to bring Him full surrender with ever-increasing intensity and totality.

The wise will allow God to bring their high and prideful places low. They also allow God to destroy their sin. They learn to live in this truth: that God has already destroyed sin's power over us. Setting all pride aside, the wise allow God to straighten what is crooked (those things that are not aligned with His Word) and smooth out the rough edges of their hearts. Can you see the progressive way of surrender now?

SURRENDERING, GOD'S WAY

Here's the problem that most of us have when it comes to surrendering to God so that we might obey His every command. We tend to try to do it in our own power. In other words, we try to surrender the flesh—by the flesh! You have already heard that nothing good resides in your flesh, yet you are probably guilty of trying to surrender by your own fleshly power anyway. You have also likely discovered that surrender by way of the flesh is fruitless. If you think that isn't true, then just think of one New Year's resolution in which you have succeeded for life!

It bears repeating. We can only accomplish surrender to God in one way—God's way! We must come to the place where we allow God to change our hearts and minds so that we understand that repentance, the intentional turning from sin that flows from a heart that God has changed, is required of every God-seeking believer. When we allow God to work in our hearts and minds, we are set free to act upon the work He has already done within us—the heart-transforming act of placing the life of Christ in us by way of the Holy Spirit. Because of this act, we can fix our gaze on Him and turn away from our sin instead. This is how we die to our flesh.

It is at the veil that divided the Inner Court from the Holy of Holies where the crucifixion of our flesh will take place. When the veil of your heart that keeps you from fully surrendering to God is removed, then you will be enabled to become a fruit-bearer of the greatest kind! But if your walk lacks crucified flesh, then your flesh will remain in its state of decline, ruling over your thoughts, words, and deeds. If you choose against the surrender that involves the crucifying of your sinful flesh, then you will become useless to God, and your "religion" will be dead. Remember, the flesh is death to you, but the Spirit is life.

God requires a response to this issue of surrender, so let's look at an Old Testament man with an incredible story of surrender. He can help us see from his example how we are to surrender. We have much to learn from this man, Abraham, and we don't have to read very far in Genesis before we see God's requirement for surrender playing out in Abraham's life. This story of Abraham's altar of death can be found in Genesis 22:1-12.

ABRAHAM'S TEST

Now it came about after these things, that God tested Abraham, and said to him, "Abraham!" And he said, "Here I am." (Genesis 22:1)

If God tested Abraham's faith, isn't it a "given" that He will test ours as well? What then was Abraham's actual test?

> *He said, "Take now your son, your only son, whom you love, Isaac, and go to the land of Moriah, and offer him there as a burnt offering on one of the mountains of which I will tell you."* (Genesis 22:2)

Did we read that correctly? Did God really tell Abraham to go up to a mountain and kill his only son, the son of the promise? Therein lies the test. Abraham dearly loved his only son, the son of his old age, the miracle boy. How could the God of love require the life of Isaac, the son He had given to Sarah and Abraham? Surely there was no greater test of Abraham's faith than that. He had plans for that son. Isaac was his pride and joy. How could God ask him to kill the one who would fulfill the promise? Yes, Abraham wanted to cling tightly to his son. But that was his flesh speaking! In his heart, he knew that he must obey.

> *So Abraham rose early in the morning and saddled his donkey, and took two of his young men with him and Isaac his son; and he split wood for the burnt offering, and arose and went to the place of which God had told him* (Genesis 22:3).

Did you notice the timeliness of Abraham's obedience? He did not linger to think about what God was asking him to do. He immediately obeyed the command of God! Though his heart surely ached, he was so sure in his spirit that God was in control that whatever questions he had were very short-lived. Abraham responded promptly by making preparations for the journey and for the altar that would be necessary if he was to obey.

> *On the third day Abraham raised his eyes and saw the place from a distance* (Genesis 22:4).

Abraham could clearly see Mount Moriah in front of him. He knew it well. That would be the place of death for his son. Unless God intervened, this was the place where his heart would be forever broken. Nonetheless, Abraham set his gaze on that place of death. Before taking Isaac there, he had a few things to say to the men traveling with them.

Abraham said to his young men, "Stay here with the donkey, and I and the lad will go over there; and we will worship and return to you." (Genesis 22:5)

Abraham knew that no matter the outcome, obeying God's command was an act of worship, and that true worship would always require a sacrifice. So, leaving the young men behind, Abraham set out to go to the mountain to worship with his beloved son. And they took with them everything that Abraham would need to do what God had asked of him.

Abraham took the wood of the burnt offering and laid it on Isaac his son, and he took in his hand the fire and the knife. So the two of them walked on together (Genesis 22:6).

Isaac, the sacrifice, carried the weightier burden. He carried the wood (even as Jesus carried His own cross) while his father carried the means to start the fire and the knife he would use to kill his own son. Then the father and son walked together up the mountain.

Isaac spoke to Abraham his father and said, "My father!" And he said, "Here I am, my son." And he said, "Behold, the fire and the wood, but where is the lamb for the burnt offering?" (Genesis 22:7)

Isaac was astute. Knowing that they were going to build an altar and offer up an animal as a burnt offering, he noticed that something was lacking—the sacrifice. So as they were walking along the way, he asked his father a logical question—what are we going to sacrifice today?

Abraham said, "God will provide for Himself the lamb for the burnt offering, my son." So the two of them walked on together (Genesis 22:8).

The word *"provide"* here means *"see"*[4] in Hebrew. God could clearly "see" the one that was to be sacrificed. That will make more sense in just a moment.

ABRAHAM'S EXAMPLE

Then they came to the place of which God had told him; and Abraham built the altar there and arranged the wood, and bound his son Isaac and laid him on the altar, on top of the wood (Genesis 22:9).

Still knowing that God was in control, Abraham arrived at the spot where the altar would be built. He set about to obediently do all that was required of him, including binding his son and laying him on top of the perfectly stacked wood.

Abraham stretched out his hand and took the knife to slay his son (Genesis 22:10).

What was he thinking at that very moment? Only God knows what ran through Abraham's mind as he raised his knife to bring his precious son's life to an end. But whatever he was thinking, God saw clearly an obedient and surrendered heart—a heart that would put to death that which was utterly precious to him. Abraham trusted God enough to slay what he held so dear.

But the angel of the Lord called to him from heaven and said, "Abraham, Abraham!" And he said, "Here I am." (Genesis 22:11)

What relief! What his heart had planned to carry out was stopped— just at the moment that his obedience was at its highest level! How incredibly sweet the angel's next words must have been to Abraham!

He said, "Do not stretch out your hand against the lad, and do nothing to him; for now I know that you fear God, since you have not withheld your son, your only son, from Me." (Genesis 22:12)

God had looked into the heart of a man who would literally love his only son to death and saw that his reverence (fear) for his God was greater than his reverence and love for the miracle child of his very old age. Oh, the smile that was surely covering the face of God! Abraham had willingly gone to the mountain of sacrifice and death to worship his God and withheld nothing from Him. And Abraham passed the test! He loved God so much that he obeyed His most difficult command. Abraham's heart of worship and surrender was the sacrifice that God was looking for. The very thing that God "saw," Abraham's obedient and surrendered heart, was the sacrifice that God required. The ram in the thicket was still sacrificed even though God's requirement had already been satisfied by Abraham's obedient surrender.

Love of God + Obedience to Him = Worship of Him! Did you know that these three words—*love, obey, and worship*—are used together for the very first time in this passage of Scripture? Isn't it amazing what God will do to make His point? We would be as wise as Abraham if we grasp how the three work together!

PERSONAL INTROSPECTION

This story is one of ultimate surrender to the Lord. And it will become an even more impacting story if we press on to see its implications for us today. In each verse, there are practical truths for us to see, understand, and apply to our journey. Let's see what we can glean from this Bible story so that we, too, can learn to surrender our hearts and lives to God with the faith of Abraham. Again, let's consider the first 12 verses of Genesis 22, with an eye on our own hearts. Let these questions pierce your heart. Answer them honestly before God. Let your heart's cry lead you to your knees and to surrender.

- God surely will test your faith. You are in the midst of a test of your faith if you are working your way through this book. Will you trust God to lead you to real surrender?

- Think back to the heart diagram that you filled out in Chapter 6. What specific sin or idol has the Lord brought to your mind? Do you understand that He is testing your faith right now as He asks you to sacrifice it on an altar of death?

- Abraham's obedient response was immediate. He did not put off what God told him to do, nor question His authority to ask for such compliance. How many times has God already asked you to lay down your particular sin or idol? Are you questioning His authority and wisdom in your life to lay it down? Or will you respond as Abraham did and immediately begin to order your life as one who is preparing to surrender?

- Your "Mount Moriah," the place of death to your flesh and sins, should be right before your eyes right now. But are you focusing on that mountain or have you turned your sights back toward what has been so comfortable for you?

- Do you consider your surrender, the offering up of your sin or idol on an altar of death, an act of worship? Do you understand that God does?

- Just as the "weightier burden" was placed on Isaac, the idols and sins that you worship are weighing you down, as well. When will your burden be lifted? When will you choose to lay it down on the altar of death, your altar of surrender? Are you willing to lay it down right now?

- Do you see that the surrender of your sin and idols and your repentance is the very burnt offering and sacrifice that God requires of you? It is the "lamb" that Isaac knew was necessary.

- Do you remember the Hebrew definition for the word *"provide"*? It means "see." God sees every sin and idol in your heart. He sees what you need to sacrifice in order for you to surrender. What He sees are the very things you are to be surrendering and putting to death. What does He see in you that He wants you, desires you, and requires you to surrender to Him? Will you?

- What will it take for you to go the mountain, build that altar, and lay your sacrifice on it? Do you realize that you will have to do more than just go through the motions of building this altar? You will have to carry through by truly laying your sacrifice down and slaying it.

- Abraham's offering would have meant nothing to God if he never intended to actually slay Isaac. Do you intend to take vengeance on your sins and idols by utterly destroying them? Will you put them to death completely? Will the Word, prayer, and reliance on the Spirit be the "knives" you raise against your sins?

- What will God have to see in you before He can tell you that you have passed His test? Do you love and reverence

Him enough to surrender your sin life and follow Him? Will you allow Him to see in you a heart of worship that is surrendered? God will respond to you in kind when you lay down your sins in surrender. Oh, how He loves it when His children lay down their lives and wills for His.

GOD'S CALL TO SURRENDER

Take a moment now to remind yourself of the definition of surrender. See for certain that surrendering is not a negative thing when it comes to your relationship with God. It is the most positive thing you can do. It is also the one discipline that will catapult you into a true love relationship with God. Surrender is giving God possession and power over your will, your desires, your goals and dreams, and your whole heart. It is yielding to Him and His commands. When you surrender in a particular area of your life, in a chamber of your heart, you give up your selfish desire to do as you wish. Surrender is the resignation of your flesh. And that leads you to a place where you can joyfully come under the power and control of the Holy Spirit. Surrender was graphically described to you in the story of Abraham and his altar of death. His test of obedience and surrender was a part of his growth in the Lord, and it will be a part of our growth as well.

Second Chronicles 7:13-14 also points us to surrender as a way of worship. Though it is often quoted on patriotic holidays as a call for our country to turn back to God for revival, these verses are specific to God's Body as well, and maybe even more specific to the individual believer. Read through them and take note of the verbs that the Lord uses as He speaks to us. Notice that they demand action. Pay close attention also to the events that surround God's call to us to worship. They are found in verse 13.

> *If I shut up the heavens so that there is no rain, or if I command the locust to devour the land, or if I send pestilence among My people....*

God may be allowing some very difficult circumstances to touch your life, and He is waiting for you to surrender to Him. Maybe they are the result of your sin and idolatry. Or maybe they are being allowed simply to bring you to the end of yourself. Either way, our call is the same. We are to surrender.

If you have ever wondered what it is that you have to do when you surrender, verse 14 will clear up any confusion you may have experienced.

And My people who are called by My name humble themselves and pray and seek My face and turn from their wicked ways, then I will hear from heaven, will forgive their sin and will heal their land.

God does not ask you to simply say a prayer in which you just tell Him that you are surrendering a sin or idol to Him. He expects you to live out Second Chronicles 7:14 by humbling yourself before the Creator of the Universe. You are to talk to Him about your sins and idols. You are to seek His face by surrendering your will. As we seek Him, we discover afresh and anew the call to obey Him. If we constantly gaze into the eyes of the Savior who offered Himself as the ultimate sacrifice and model of surrender, how could our response be anything but repentance? Turning away from what is sinful in our lives is entirely different than merely telling God how sorry we are that we have sinned and asking for His forgiveness. It is doing a 180-degree turn, away from the direction we had been heading. This is surrender! This is true worship!

God has called us to a repentant, heart-surrendering concert of prayer, to be on our faces before Him, the One whose very face we seek. Until we find ourselves prostrate before Him, we will continue to wander in our self-made wildernesses, stagnant and unfulfilled, never reaching the "land" that He has promised us. Surrender is the key to passing through the "veil" and into the daily presence and will of God!

THE TRUTH ABOUT OUR WITNESS

Let's take a brief look now at the first two verses of Romans 12. They can open our minds, as well, to the truth of the story of Abraham's surrender. Just like Abraham was asked to sacrifice his own flesh and blood, Isaac his only son, we have an altar of death that we must face. And the sacrifice is to be our flesh. These two verses describe it well.

Therefore I urge you, brethren, by the mercies of God, to present your bodies a living and holy sacrifice, acceptable to God, which is your spiritual service of worship (Romans 12:1).

God is asking for our crucified flesh when He urges us to be living sacrifices. You might be asking what your flesh actually is. What is God asking for? Your flesh is made up of the body, the mind, our intent, and our thoughts. Our flesh is anything that stands in opposition to what God says. And this is what God asks of us: to put to death anything that is unacceptable to Him. This is what He defines as worship.

And do not be conformed to this world, but be transformed by the renewing of your mind, so that you may prove what the will of God is, that which is good and acceptable and perfect (Romans 12:2).

This is a huge problem with Christians today. We don't look any different, in most cases, than those who are not believers. The world can barely tell the difference, if at all. We do not stand out. We blend in. We are conformed to the world when we watch the same television shows and movies that the world watches. We are conformed to the world when our CDs, iPods, and radios pump the same kind of music into our minds and hearts that the world listens to. We dress like the world, talk like the world, and think like the world. We take firm hold of the reins of our lives every morning when we wake up, and we don't lay them down until we fall into bed at night. We continue doing what we know is wrong to do. We want the same things that the godless want—more money, bigger homes, all the newest toys—security in all the wrong things. We often are independent, self-sufficient, multitasking people who have no need for a God who wants to take away our control.

Jesus will never be the *Lord* of the lost because they have yet to receive Him as their Savior. We believers tend to accept Him readily as our Savior, yet we struggle to allow Him to be *Lord*. Quite often the only real difference between the lost and the saved is that we believe that Jesus is the Savior. Most of us do not know Him as *Lord*. We only seem to know that He is supposed to be our Lord. In actuality, for Him to be *Lord*, we would have to live in a constant state of surrender. That requires us to crucify our desire to be in control of everything in our lives.

By looking at the Greek definitions of a couple of phrases from Romans 12:1-2, we see a critical step in the walk of every believer. The true rendering of the phrase "present[5] yourselves[6]" is this: a presenting and a yielding of your whole self. Now let me ask you an important question. Were you fully surrendered at the time of your salvation? If you are like me, the answer is a resounding no! Jesus did not become the *Lord* of everything in my life the moment I was saved. He was available to be that, but on the day that I was saved, I only surrendered to Him as my Savior. I had no understanding of what it meant to know Jesus as my Lord, my Master, as the one in full control of me.

YOUR FULL SURRENDER

So, what does it mean to fully surrender? I believe it refers to a point in time when we become serious about our relationship with God and clearly understand the requirements of God for all believers. It doesn't mean that all of our sin will be magically removed from our sinful flesh, but it does mean that we are ready to give God the control of our life in such a way that we allow Him to systematically, and by spiritual surgery, remove those things that cause us to stumble and fall.

Literally, be transformed here means that to change by means of an invisible process which begins during our life on earth.[7] Interesting, isn't it? We are not to be conformed to the world, but we are to be instead constantly changing into the likeness of Christ. This is surrender and this is the spiritual service of worship that comes from the sacrificing of our flesh on the altar of death. This surrender leads to sanctification. Like Abraham, we are to worship God by loving Him enough to obey what He desires. Oswald Chambers says it this way:

> Sin belongs to hell and the devil.... It is not a question of giving up sin, but of giving up my right to myself, my natural independence and self-assertiveness, and this is where the battle has to be fought. ...To discern that natural virtues antagonize

surrender to God, is to bring our souls into the centre of its greatest battle. ...It is going to cost the natural in you everything, not something. Jesus said, "If any man will be My disciple, let him deny himself." ...Beware of refusing to go to the funeral of your own independence. ...If we do not resolutely sacrifice the natural, the supernatural can never become natural in us.[8]

Believing that Jesus is Savior and King is enough in our moment of salvation, but it is not enough the moment we desire to live the abundant life promised by Christ. We must choose to make Jesus the Lord of our lives and believe that He is in charge of our lives, making a conscious effort to surrender to Him based on that belief. The enemy loves to use the lie that salvation is enough for a transformed life. Believing that lie is one of the main reasons that so many Christians stay in the Outer Court of the Tabernacle for so many years, enjoying its ease and refusing to step into the Inner Court of surrender.

Have you experienced a full surrender to the will of God? Are you seeking to continually surrender your flesh and your will to God? Or are you like a yo-yo when it comes to your sin—you throw it out and then pull it back? When will you finally, once and for all, cut the string? What is your answer to God's call to surrender and heart transformation? Andrew Murray understood it like this, and in a public address titled "Absolute Surrender," he said, "God is ready to assume full responsibility for the life wholly yielded to Him. The condition for obtaining God's full blessing is absolute surrender to Him."[9]

If you will heed His call, you are about to see what great power from the Spirit can be released within you. Interested? Read on!

INTROSPECTION

I. When you allow your flesh to have control and make the decisions in your life, who is truly the god of your life?

2. By what actions can God and the entire world see that you are walking on the Highway to Holiness? How do your answers line up with Second Chronicles 7:14 and Romans 12:1-2?

3. How does surrender differ from making New Year's resolutions? Who is in control?

4. What part of the Tabernacle symbolizes the crucifixion of our flesh, our greatest surrender? How close are you to the Holy of Holies when you are surrendering your flesh?

5. In which areas of your heart is your surrender like a yo-yo—you throw out the sin, but it seems to keep coming back? Consider whether you have truly surrendered it.

ENDNOTES

1. Paul Aiello Jr., www.sermonillustrations.com/a-z/s/submission.htm.

2. Oswald Chambers, *My Utmost for His Highest* (Grand Rapids, MI: Discovery House Publishers, 1963), 297.

3. *Webster's New World Dictionary* (Cleveland, OH: William Collins Publishing Inc.), 1,433.

4. www.htmlbible.com/sacrednamebiblecom/kjvstrongs/CONHEB719. htm#S7200.

5. www.htmlbible.com/sacrednamebiblecom/kjvstrongs/STRGRK39.htm.

6. Zodhiates, *The Complete Word Study Dictionary: New Testament*, 1,356-7, #4983-III.

7. Zodhiates, *The Complete Word Study Dictionary: New Testament*, 969, #3339.

8. Chambers, *My Utmost for His Highest*, 344.

9. Andrew Murray, *Absolute Surrender*, Public Domain.

CHAPTER 10

THE POWER
BEYOND YOUR SURRENDER

...From his innermost being will flow rivers of living water
(John 7:38).

Bernard Shaw played the "What If" game shortly before he died. "Mr. Shaw," asked a reporter, "if you could live your life over and be anybody you've known, or any person from history, who would you be?"

"I would choose," replied Shaw "to be the man George Bernard Shaw could have been, but never was."[1]

Can't you hear the remorse in the voice of George Bernard Shaw? What was it that he regretted? His regret was in not living up to the full potential that dwelled within him. Can you relate to that? Have you lived up to your full potential as a child of God? Having looked at the topic of surrender in the previous chapter as the means of entering into the daily presence of God and walking in submission to Him by the Spirit, we now turn our attention to the vital role the Holy Spirit will play as we surrender our whole hearts to Him. When we learn to surrender every sin in our broken hearts and allow Him to live out the holy life of Christ through us, we will begin to see the message of this chapter: There is great victory and power that lies just beyond our surrender. By that power, we can become in Christ all that He intends for us and live with no regrets for who we could have been.

GOD'S PLAN APPLIED TO OUR HEARTS

Let's revisit Second Chronicles 7:13-14. We will use it now as a tool by which we can surrender to the Lordship of Jesus Christ any sin found in our hearts. Consider this a continuation of the exercises of identifying the sins and idols in our hearts from Chapter 6, taking full vengeance on them in Chapter 7, and understanding the degree to which we must follow all of God's commands in Chapter 8. Read these words very carefully.

> If...My people who are called by My name humble themselves and pray and seek My face and turn from their wicked ways, then I will hear from heaven, will forgive their sin and will heal their land.

The first thing we must do is humble ourselves before our Creator, Savior, and Lord. We can do that by making time to be with Him. We will never experience real surrender to God regarding a sin issue if we do not spend time with the One to whom we will surrender that part of our heart. Our humility will not likely reach our desired point of surrender if we do not set apart a good amount of time for that surrender. We tend to avoid the whole issue of humility before the Lord because humility stands in opposition to our god-infested, fleshly, prideful hearts. When we truly see ourselves in light of who God is, it will be humbling as well as enlightening in a way that is rarely comfortable. Here is an example. Let's say that the sin we want to surrender to God is the sin of self-sufficiency. As we come before the Lord in regard to this god, we must humbly focus on His holiness and His desire for His children to find their sufficiency in Him alone. We must be able to see clearly that we are in the wrong for having trusted in our own devices instead of trusting in the Lord first and always. This is the first step of surrender.

As you begin to pour out your heart to God in prayer, you must seek further illumination of the sin or god you are bringing to the altar of sacrifice. Sometimes you will need to see your sin in greater detail. Maybe God wants to show you the devastating effects it has had on you or others. Possibly He will want you to see how it is stifling your growth, or He may show you other sins that have grown out of that particular one. There are many things He might want to reveal to you, so you must not only pour out your sins to God but also be willing to invest some time in just listening to what He wants to tell you about them. Once God is done speaking to your heart, you can then confess it, agreeing with God that it is sin, and renounce the effects it has had on you. Then it will be a good practice to keep this sin before Him in your daily prayer times, praying for protection from its entrance back into your life. This is practicing spiritual warfare for the purpose of spiritual healing.

Once that sin has been surrendered to God, it is time to begin to truly seek God's face. If you are going to surrender a sin to God, it would be a travesty not to fill the empty place now found in your heart with the Lord Himself in the form of the Holy Spirit! If you allow Him to fill that "chamber," then He will help you to do *His* will! When you need it, He will be there to give you counsel for the new choices you will need to be making as you walk in your newfound freedom from that sin. Another way of saying this is that you will be empowered to turn from your wicked ways. With your heart's sin chamber surrendered to God and filled up with the Holy Spirit, you will find yourself forsaking what is displeasing to God and those choices that are against His will.

This is a process. It is not the end. It will take your entire lifetime to have your heart fully cleansed and healed. This is our sanctification: our perfecting, our maturing as Christians, and our completeness in Him.

SACRIFICES THAT DELIGHT GOD

But now we have to turn our focus to what will happen when we do surrender our sinful hearts to God. Our surrender will lead to victory, perseverance, and power! If we lack power and victory in our daily walk, we can most assuredly know that our personal surrender is lacking.

Psalm 51:16-17 sheds some more light on just what kind of sacrifice God requires of us when we surrender.

> *For You do not delight in sacrifice, otherwise I would give it; You are not pleased with burnt offering. The sacrifices of God are a broken spirit; a broken and a contrite heart, O God, You will not despise.*

God wants our hearts and spirits to be broken by our sin. He is looking for a broken and contrite heart in the one who comes to a place of total surrender. This brokenness and contriteness must be so intense that it leads to real repentance, the turning away from that sin and toward the God of our heart. This kind of brokenness is a deep sorrow and remorse for our sinfulness that is followed by the desire to never fall prey to that sin ever again. Broken means to "to break or crush into pieces"[2] and contrite means "to collapse[3]"!

Is that how you have taken full vengeance on your sin in the past? Have you ever been to that place? Have you been broken to pieces by your sin? Or have you ever collapsed from following after your sinful flesh, the very gods of your life? It is difficult in our pridefulness to get to that place of contriteness and brokenness. We will try every form of evasion to avoid being ground to pieces, and believe me, I know that from my own experiences! True surrender and repentance are rare in the church today, it seems. Yet we cannot offer God the correct sacrifice if we aren't broken and contrite. Have you ever found yourself saying any of these following phrases, as I have?

- "I don't need to do that because I'm already forgiven."

- "I am not all that affected by my sin."

- "Who cares anyway?"

- "I don't want to be labeled as a radical Christian."

- "I'm afraid that if I fully surrender, God will make me do something that I'm uncomfortable with."

Maybe the enemy has spoken things to you that are different than these. It doesn't really matter what he has spoken to you; they are still excuses if you listen to them and use them.

SATAN'S DECEPTION

Do you know what all these excuses are? They are lies and deception from an enemy who would love for us to remain unyielded to God. He stands to gain territory in our hearts if he can keep us from submitting to God's call for surrender. If he can make us believe for any reason that we don't need to take our sin seriously, then he will be thrilled to keep us from the power that is available to all who do surrender to God's full control. He would love for us to never surrender anything to God! He would love to continue to hold us captive in our sin! He wants to keep us from victory.

The Bible, however, says very clearly to us in Galatians 6:7: *"Do not be deceived, God is not mocked; for whatever a man sows, this he will also reap."*

Do you see what your response is to be? God is calling you to surrender your sins and turn from them. You are not to be deceived by the lies of the devil. If you continue to make excuses for not surrendering and repenting, God will say to you, "I will not be mocked!" When you choose to sow for yourselves the seeds of denial of your sin and its influence, you will reap a bitter fruit of defeat. But if you sow for yourself the seeds of repentance and surrender, from a heart that is broken and contrite, you will necessarily produce a different kind of fruit. That fruit is victory over your sin and a powerful life in the Spirit that you will never know unless you turn from your sin and allow Him full control of your life. Victory and power lie just around the corner for the one who will lay down the boastful pride of life for the purpose of surrendering to God's authority. Persevering victory and power are the gifts of God for the truly heartbroken, surrendered servants of the Lord.

The Artesian Well

Several years ago, God gave me a picture of part of His creation that reveals one of His spiritual principles so clearly. I love it when He does that! This natural world we live in will often paint us a picture of the spiritual realm. The picture He painted for me was that of an artesian well. Study for a moment the picture of the artesian well. It should help you visualize the truths to follow.

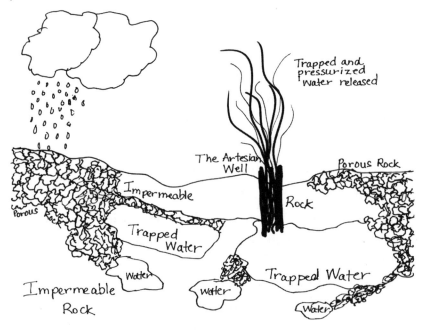

You might be asking yourself the question, "What is an artesian well?" I asked myself the same question when it was presented in our homeschool curriculum in science. In order to teach it, I had to know exactly what it was. I did a little research in the encyclopedia, but I found a form of this simple picture in a set of children's science reference books. As I looked at the picture, the explanation, and a definition from *Webster's Dictionary*, it was not very long before I sensed God speaking to my soul regarding the artesian well as a picture of our repentance, but even more as a picture of the power of surrender!

Let's get a good working understanding of an artesian well. Like all wells, its water is reached by boring into the earth. But by God's design, an artesian well, when the drilling reaches the water, sprays up like a fountain with great power because it is under great pressure beneath the ground. Now that you know that, does the picture make a little more sense? Doesn't it look like a geyser?

So just how is an artesian well created? It all begins with rain. Rain hits the ground and permeates the surface. Usually an artesian well is formed beneath layers of rock, the first layer being porous rock. The water passes through the holes in the rock quickly and easily, moving downward as it seeks the lowest level by the path of least resistance. It fills every hole it finds. It continues its downward advance until it reaches the lowest level. There it is trapped between layers of impermeable rock, and there it is kept contained until heavy machinery is used to bore deeply through the impermeable rock. Once the drill reaches the pressurized water, it spews forth, shooting upward with great power and force. It truly does resemble a geyser as it explodes upward.

Now here's where it gets fun! Looking at the spiritual application we can glean from the artesian well, we can then fill in the blanks on the diagram. The symbolism is quite apparent. Let it minister to you as you see the perfection of God's picture of the power of your surrender.

1. The Holy Spirit indwells us at the time of our salvation. He rains down on us from Heaven and comes into our very hearts, His Tabernacle. He takes the path of least resistance, filling up the holes of our sin-ravaged lives.

2. Once inside of us, our fleshly, sinful pride traps Him, so He resides deep within us, waiting to be released by our full surrender to His authority and control. We know His power is there inside of us, but we don't see it exploding forth in our lives, and neither does anyone else. Our pride is what keeps us from surrendering fully to His Lordship.

3. When we decide to bring in the heavy equipment of repentance and surrender, a deep boring takes place within

our hearts. This repentance and surrender breaks through what has been our impermeable sin and pride. Once our repentance and brokenness go deep enough, the Holy Spirit is released in us and out of us like a powerful fountain. He shoots upward to the Father, glorifying Him and granting us power and victory over our sin. Then others will experience the power of our surrender as we begin to walk under the influence of the Spirit instead of our flesh and sin nature. They will see the "new and greatly improved" us!

It is the rain in the diagram that is the Holy Spirit. In the Word, the Spirit is often spoken of as water. The porous rock is the sin in our lives. It is all the holes in our sinful hearts that are obvious before we know the Lord. But then, as is often the case, the Holy Spirit becomes trapped inside of us by the impermeable rock of our fleshly pride and daily sin. The Holy Spirit is now rendered powerless because we refuse to allow Him to have full control of our lives. Do you see how our brokenness over sin and the repentance and surrender that follows is the drill that is necessary for the Spirit to come forth from us in power? Without our repentance and surrender to the Spirit, He lies trapped inside of us with nowhere to go. He is the power inside of us that we have been given to be all that God intended for us to be. When He is not released from us by our surrender, we live powerless lives that are without victory over our sin. In this state, we will surely die and stand before the Lord with regrets for not having become the person God desired and empowered us to be.

Awesome, isn't it? Can you now more easily see now how it is that you can walk in the power of the Spirit if you are broken, repentant, and surrendered to God? Can you share this principle with others who might need to know how to set the Spirit inside of them free? What a great visual to share with those who ask you what has happened to you and how it is that you have changed. It is by the power of the Spirit in you that has been released out of you by your surrender to the perfect will of God!

RIVERS OF LIVING WATER

Consider your life right now. Do you desire to be pleasing to the Lord by bringing Him your sacrifice of surrender now? If so, let these next three passages shed new light on the artesian well of surrender. They will clearly reveal the life rewards that await the one who is submitted to the power of the Holy Spirit within:

> *Therefore you will joyously draw water from the springs of salvation* (Isaiah 12:3).

> *Jesus answered and said to her, "Everyone who drinks of this water will thirst again; but whoever drinks of the water that I will give him shall never thirst; but the water that I will give him will become in him a well of water springing up to eternal life"* (John 4:13-14).

> *"He who believes in Me, as the Scripture said, 'From his innermost being will flow rivers of living water.'" But this He spoke of the Spirit, whom those who believed in Him were to receive; for the Spirit was not yet given, because Jesus was not yet glorified* (John 7:38-39).

God is so specific, isn't He? But let's not just revel in the wonderful thought of what can be. Let's take the thought one more step—into action! We must apply this truth by contemplating our own lives. Do you have sin in your life that you are holding onto, sin that is keeping God's power trapped inside you? Has your pride kept you from giving over all of your sin habits to the God who desires to explode forth from you? Do you understand clearly now that repentance and surrender are the only tools that will enable you to bore deeply into your heart, bringing you to victorious, overcoming power in your life? Are you ready now for the Holy Spirit to flow out of you to others, touching them with His living waters? Do you care about unleashing the Spirit that is trapped inside of you? And do you realize that in your lifetime, there will be many such borings of repentance and surrender? Surrender was never intended to be a "once and for all" deal. It will be a continual process during your walk toward Heaven.

Your understanding and application of surrender of your whole heart will determine the amount of power that can be witnessed in your life. If you seek to overcome by the power of the Spirit, then you must find the altar of death and the surrender that can only be found at the veil of the Tabernacle. That is the place where your flesh dies.

I would like to close with a prayer that I found many years ago. It is a powerful prayer and has led me in my own surrender on more than one occasion. To pray it without conviction will not yield the fruit of repentance. But this prayer prayed with a broken and contrite heart will help you to humble yourself before the Lord. Once humbled you can bring in the heavy machinery of surrender and repentance so that the Spirit can be unleashed in you and out of you! There is now no need for prayers that beg, "Give me strength, Lord." The Holy Spirit is all the strength you need, and He lives inside of you! His strength is already ours if we will yield to Him and die to the fleshly emotions of fear, doubt, and dread. If you are ready now to begin the deep drilling process of repentance and surrender, then pray this prayer out loud. . .on your knees or on your face before the Lord God.

Lord, I'm Yours. Whatever the cost may be, may Your will be done in my life. I realize I'm not here on earth to do my own thing, or to seek my own fulfillment, or my own glory. I'm not here to indulge my desires, to increase my possessions, to impress people, to be popular, to prove I'm somebody important, or to promote myself. I'm not even here to be relevant or successful by human standards. I'm here to please You.

I offer myself to You, for You are worthy. All that I am or hope to be, I owe to You. I'm Yours by creation, and every day I receive from You life and breath and all things. And I am Yours because You bought me, and the price You paid was the precious blood of Christ. You alone are worthy to be my Lord and Master. I yield to You, my gracious and glorious Heavenly Father; to the Lord Jesus who loved me and gave Himself for me; to the Holy Spirit and His gracious influence and empowering.

All that I am and all that I have I give to You. I give You any rebellion in me that resists doing Your will. I give You my pride and self-dependence that tell me I can do Your will in my own power if I try hard enough. I give You my fears that tell me I'll never be able to do Your will in some areas of my life. I consent to let You energize me. . .to create within me, moment by moment, both the desire and the power to do Your will.

I give You my body and each of its members...my entire inner being: my mind, my emotional life, my will...my loved ones...my marriage or my hopes for marriage...my abilities and gifts... my strengths and weaknesses...my health...my status (high or low)...my possessions...my past, my present, and my future...and when and how I'll go Home. I am here to love You, to obey You, and to glorify You. O my Beloved, may I be a joy to You[4] Amen and Amen!

INTROSPECTION

1. What is the one sacrifice, mentioned in Psalm 51:16-17, that God requires of you?

2. What is standing in the way of your humble and contrite surrender to God?

3. Prideful sin keeps the Holy Spirit trapped inside of us. The drilling of our "artesian well" will allow the Spirit to unleash His power through us. What does the artesian well symbolize?

4. What are the specific sins that are keeping the Holy Spirit trapped inside of you?

5. How willing are you to surrender and repent of your sins, so that you may experience the power of the Holy Spirit in your life?

ENDNOTES

1. Nido R. Qubein, www.sermonillustrations.com/a-z/p/potential.htm.

2. www.htmlbible.com/sacrednamebiblecom/kjvstrongs/STRHEB76.htm#S7665.

3. www.htmlbible.com/sacrednamebiblecom/kjvstrongs/STRHEB17.htm#S1794.

4. Warren and Ruth Myers, *31 Days of Praise* (Sisters, OR: Multnomah Publisher Inc., 1994), 155-57.

CHAPTER 11

ENDURING THE JOURNEY

For you have need of endurance, so that when you have done the will of God, you may receive what was promised (Hebrews 10:36).

The Greeks had a race in their Olympic games that was unique. The winner was not the runner who finished first. It was the runner who finished with his torch still lit. I want to run all the way with the flame of my torch still lit for Him.[1] That is exactly what God is looking for: the lit torches of His children as they finish their journeys on earth. But just how will we endure this race, this life of learning surrender and obedience, in such a way that our torches are not extinguished? The answer lies in what we focus on.

WHERE WE HAVE BEEN

If we have been making spiritual adjustments during the previous chapters, then we are well into the journey of our lifetime. This journey has taken us through Moses' Tabernacle, learning how it relates to our journey toward Christlikeness and how to appropriate its applicable truths to our spiritual lives. The Tabernacle, being likened to our hearts, the very place where God now resides, was a tool we used, not only for discovering where we currently stand on this journey to wholeheartedness on this earth, but also for plotting the journey to our Heavenly home.

But the Tabernacle left us with some questions. We discovered that we were at a crossroads. Knowing where we are at leads us on to a choice as to which direction we would be traveling. The crossroads was an opportunity for us to clearly understand that we must consider our ways so that we might choose the correct spiritual paths for our lives. But that chapter left us with yet another question—just how do we continually choose the right path?

That question forced us to take a better look at our hearts, the Tabernacle of God. If we were to consider our ways, it was critical that we take a magnifying glass to what "our ways" have actually been. By writing on our cracked and damaged hearts, we soon discovered that "our ways" have been bound up in gods, the sins that we bow down to and worship. I doubt that anyone's filled-in heart was a pretty picture. I know that mine horrified me as I realized "in black and white" just how sinful a place my heart was. It saddened me, as I am sure it did you, to see the gods that replaced Jesus on the throne of my heart.

But it was not going to be enough to just identify what was keeping us out of the Holy of Holies. Something had to be done with our hearts. God definitely needed to be placed in the center of our hearts, or we would surely fail. Our attempts without God will always end up just exactly like our feeble attempts at New Year's resolutions! As we returned to the Word, we discovered that God had a plan for us to dispossess the gods of our hearts by taking full vengeance on them. They had to be dethroned! It was the answer to yet another unspoken question.

What makes taking full vengeance on our sins and gods so difficult is that we are prone to disobey the commands of God, even when they are clearly spelled out for us. We learned that there are spiritual consequences for not fully following all that God has commanded us to do. The only way to be obedient is to understand and practice the discipline of surrender. Surrender is where all the power lies! Our life goal should be to live surrendered to the Lord Jesus Christ!

The words and lessons found in this book are meant to encourage and admonish you on your journey to a healed heart, a heart that is single-minded and single in purpose, aiming to please and imitate Jesus by our surrender and obedience. Wouldn't it be great if it only required just one choice for obedience or even just a day of it? The problem is this: our journey here on earth is long when one considers the number of times we will be called to be obedient! So let's look at how we can endure the journey by examining some important points in the Book of Hebrews.

OUR FAITHFUL EXAMPLES

We will be taking an in-depth look at Hebrews 12:1-4, but before we begin our study of that passage, I remind you that it is important to read the Word in context. It is always a good practice when you are studying the Word to look at the chapter or a few verses before and after what you plan to study. This will often give great insight into your passage of study.

The chapter just ahead of Hebrews 12:1-4 is the chapter I have often heard referred to as the "Christian Heroes Hall of Fame" or "The Faithful Who's Who List" for all who aspire to be faithful followers of Jesus. It is filled with the brief stories of the faith of the likes of Abel, Enoch, Noah, Abraham, Sarah, Isaac, Jacob, Joseph, Moses, Joshua, Rahab, Gideon, Barak, Samson, Jephthah, David, Samuel, and the prophets.

This chapter tells us of the accomplishments of faith and obedience. It tells us of the many who have gone before us who walked in faith and gained God's approval. It is a chapter full of miracles and hardships. And this chapter is about the lineage of every believer. It is about the legacy that has been left for us and from which we are to learn and then imitate. Hebrews 11 is a list of our great cloud of witnesses!

But Hebrews 12 will cause us to ask ourselves just what kind of legacy we want to leave for those who will come after us! Read it below.

> *Therefore, since we have so great a cloud of witnesses surrounding us, let us also lay aside every encumbrance and the sin which so easily entangles us, and let us run with endurance the race that is set before us, fixing our eyes on Jesus, the author and perfecter of faith, who for the joy set before Him endured the cross, despising the shame, and has sat down at the right hand*

of the throne of God. For consider Him who has endured such hostility by sinners against Himself, so that you will not grow weary and lose heart. You have not yet resisted to the point of shedding blood in your striving against sin.... (Hebrews 12:1-4).

Did you notice the "let us" phrases? Whenever you come across a "let us" verse, you need to read it as "I must." It is a gentle command; it is not a suggestion! What did the "let us" phrases tell us to do?

1. Lay aside every encumbrance and the sin that so easily entangles us.

2. Run with endurance the race that is set before us.

If you have been in church, participated in Sunday school, attended a small group, or just read your Bible, you know that eventually you will hear or see something that has to do with how we are to be dealing with our sin. But in this chapter we are going to discover our need to deal with *all* things that hinder our walk. We are going to use the Greek definitions of certain words in our passage to give us a clearer understanding of what Hebrews 12:1-4 actually means to us and what was originally intended by its author. Read these four verses now.

LAYING ASIDE EVERY ENCUMBRANCE

Let's take a closer look now at some very important words in this text.

• Lay aside—to put away, cast off, lay down, put off, the opposite of storing up[2]

Can you think of any examples of "storing up"? I like to create word pictures. They help me "see" better what is meant by certain words. That's how visual learners learn best! Here are my word pictures: "a well-stocked pantry," "grain bins too full for even one more kernel of corn," and "fat stores." (I know—don't remind you!) Things that are used to store up other things are designed with a plan and purpose for "storing up." There is no other reason for it! So, if "laying aside" means the opposite of "storing up," then we need a plan and a purpose for "laying aside" every encumbrance that we have as well as the sin that entangles us on our Christian walk.

- Every encumbrance—a burden, hindrance, or weight; specific to this verse, it means a tumor, mass, impediment, a stumbling block[3]

It is critical that you understand this definition because an encumbrance and a sin are defined as different things. The encumbrances that the writer of Hebrews is referring to are *not* those things that are clearly defined as sin. He covers that in the next phrase of our passage, and we will define "sin" next. So what is he referring to? Encumbrances are those stumbling blocks that are often called the "gray areas" of the Bible. An encumbrance can be anything that impedes your walk that isn't specifically identified as sin. Consider these: too much television, smoking, drinking, and being a workaholic. Do you get the picture?

The word "encumbrance" concerns those things that weigh you down or hinder you from doing what God wants you to be doing. Often you justify their presence in your life because the Word doesn't say that they are sin to you. Yet they rob you of certain aspects of your relationship with God and eventually burden you. What do you depend or rely upon other than God? What do you do that creates a way for you to spend more time with it than you do with God, often excluding Him from your daily life? These are stumbling blocks intentionally set in your way by our enemy. Here is a specific example of a stumbling block in the Word.

In Matthew 16, Jesus had just told the disciples of the real events that were about to happen in Jerusalem. Jesus' prediction of His death gave them more details than had been disclosed during their previous discussions. Peter couldn't handle the truth he had just heard. Jesus told them that He was about to die, and Peter's rebuke was strong. But it was filled with adoration for his Master. In his blurting sort of way, Peter boldly told Jesus that His death would never happen! Jesus immediately turned to address Peter, saying, *"Get behind Me, Satan!"* (Matt. 16:23). Jesus understood that the thoughts of Peter had been infiltrated by the enemy.

So Jesus said, *"You are a stumbling block to Me; for you are not setting your mind on God's interests, but man's"* (Matt. 16:23).

You see, your own thoughts that are self-absorbed, self-centered, and self-focused can just as easily be a stumbling block to you or to someone else. They are flesh-fed thoughts, and satan delights in such thoughts, for they do not consider the thoughts of God. If you struggle with these kinds of thoughts, your battle plan to overcome them is found in the verses that follow the account of Peter's wrong thinking.

> *Then Jesus said to His disciples, "If anyone wishes to come after Me, he must deny himself, and take up his cross, and follow Me"* (Matthew 16:24).

This is the answer not only to self-centered thinking but also for every sin you will battle. We must learn to simply tell our flesh no! By denying ourselves what our flesh wants, we "take up the cross," for that is what Jesus did when He clearly understood what His Father's will was. If we tell ourselves no and then obey what God says, in any given situation, then we are following Him. Those things that encumber us are stumbling blocks and often appear to be innocent activities, but we trip over them all the time. What activity is currently encumbering your walk?

THE SIN THAT EASILY ENTANGLES

- And the sin—missing the true end and scope of our lives, which is God, an offense with emphasis on guilt.[4]

These are the actions, attitudes, and words that we know are wrong and oppose God's Word. No discussion is needed here. We know what they are!

- Entangles—a picture of a competitor trying to thwart a racer from every direction[5]; easily surrounding, and can lead to calamity.[6]

Wasn't that a great picture of entangling? You are trying to run the race of your life, but your competitor, the devil, is doing everything within his power and from every direction to trip you up! Let's take what we have learned now and create a new verse, one based on the Greek definitions that are original to the text.

> Since I have been shown such great examples of people in the Bible who learned how to walk out their faith, and they now surround me, I choose to get rid of my storehouses of stumbling blocks that have been hindering my walk. I choose also to put away the things I do and say and think that I know are in direct opposition to God. These encumbrances and sins are intended by the competitor of my faith to surround me and cause me to trip so that I will be disqualified from the race. I now understand that I am being led to calamity when I continue in my sin and encumbrances. Both can entangle me as they surround me. I choose to walk surrounded in the faith of those who have gone before me.

The faithful ones who were listed in the Heroes Hall of Fame are the ones who successfully put their sins and encumbrances behind them while marching on in the faith and obedience of those who have been called by God. Had they not done this, they wouldn't have been included in God's great list. They are our examples and legacy. Therefore, we should follow suit.

RUNNING WITH ENDURANCE

Let's define now the important words of the second phrase containing "let us."

- Run—run or walk hastily having a course to run; specifically here "with strenuous effort."[7]

Can you sense the urgency and intensity of this kind of running? This kind of run will not be easy or leisurely. The course referred to has already been set for us by God. And we will need endurance to finish the race.

- Endurance—patient continuing (waiting when necessary), bearing up under the strain with a tranquil mind, not surrendering to them (the sin and encumbrances).[8]

Wow! I had no idea that my endurance required a tranquil mind set only on the hope of making it through! I am not sure I have ever correctly endured! But we must not miss the other words in the definition. To endure will require something in me that says that I will keep going no matter what. I must stay the course with a constancy that patiently continues when it is difficult as well as when it is easy. This race is about learning to be obedient in all things. When the Word speaks of not surrendering to those things that can entangle me, I must decide now to bear up when temptations, trials, and tests come so that I can win the race by gaining victories over them. And that leads us right into the next Greek definition.

- The race—strife, contention, a struggle, a contest for victory or mastery, a contest against the enemies of man's salvation, much like the Greek games.[9]

Because satan wishes to thwart our effort to gain victory or mastery over our sin and stumbling blocks, our fight with him will require great effort. Our enemy wants to keep us in our sin, maybe more than we want to be free of it. Therefore, he will contend with us with every weapon in his arsenal. We must learn to use our full armor, and specifically the sword of the Spirit, with even more effort and zeal than satan uses on us.

Do you see now why it is so very important to understand our Bibles in their original language? The Greek must define its own words in the New Testament; our English dictionaries just cannot get the job done!

OUR RACE

Putting all of those definitions together we will see in an "amplified" way what Hebrews 12:1 really is telling us.

Considering that God has designed for us a particular race to run where we are to lay aside the things that trip us up on our journey to Him, we should set our minds on giving the race a strenuous effort so as never to surrender to our stumbling blocks and sins. We should attack this race as our course on earth, one of mastery and victory over satan and sin.

If we do not live out this verse in our daily walk of obedience to God, our sins and our encumbrances will keep us from a walk of faith that could influence others. Have you considered what effect your sin and "allowances" have had on those around you? What impact could it have if you continue in your disobedience? Do you remember the legacy left to us by the great cloud of witnesses? What legacy do you really want to leave? Do you want your legacy to be that you tolerated your own disobedience to your Creator while He abhorred it or that you fought the good fight, that you ran a great race, that led you to the surrender that brought victory into your life?

GETTING BACK ON TRACK

Do you find that you now have a course correction to make? The masterful author of Hebrews has the "how to" in verse 2 of Hebrews 12. He says to "fix your eyes on Jesus" because He is the Author and Perfecter of faith. With our eyes fixed on Him, He will lead us to the perfecting of our faith. Our faith began at our salvation with Jesus and our belief in Him. Though we are a character in the book He is writing of our faith walk, He is the Author of it, not us! He is also the One who is doing the perfecting in us. We would never be capable of heart transformation on our own!

Again, what do the "let us" phrases tell us to do?

- Lay aside what is holding us back.

- Run with endurance.

The laying aside of our sin and encumbrances is a call to Lordship. As we begin to walk in the Spirit and lay aside our stumbling blocks, we are actually making Jesus the Lord of those particular areas. We are giving Him His rightful seat in our hearts, which allows Him full control over the things that can entangle us and get us off course.

THE ENDURANCE OF CHRIST, OUR EXAMPLE

Our call to holiness will require from us a run of endurance, a race in which we do not waver but continue to obey no matter what trial, temptation, or test comes our way. And lest we think such laying aside and endurance is impossible, we need only look to Jesus. He is the One on whom we must focus our sights while we run this race. He is our ultimate example and witness because He has endured the cross.

This is what Jesus did when He endured: He endured our hostility while we were sinners. He walked in the shame that we deserved. As His children, now we can endure our trials without becoming weary and losing heart. Now we have the power to attack our sin issues by obedience to the Word in full surrender to the One who showed us how to endure. Have you ever considered that? Jesus endured on the cross for us so that we might endure as we take a stand against our most besetting sins and stumbling blocks today. And He did it by focusing on the joy that was ahead of Him, His triumphant return to the Father and His eternal home. Should we be focusing on anything else but Christ and eternity in Heaven? By setting our focus on Him, we can endure until we gain triumphant victory over sin.

We will never endure as completely as Jesus did, for He resisted to the point of shedding blood. Even if we persevere in surrender and obedience, we will never work so hard as to shed blood as Jesus did. No one has or will ever resist sin to that degree. But it is still our duty and our responsibility to be about the removal of sin and stumbling blocks from our Christian walk with the desire to overcome, master, and gain victory over what satan has used to entangle us.

Finally, I'll share one more insight from the Greek definition for "run." It compels me to run more diligently, and I hope you will find it equally compelling. This word "run" is used to compare, figuratively, the public races of biblical times to Christians and their call to a strenuous, godly life.[10]

This race, this course that has been set for us by God Himself, which allows for the weeding out of sin and encumbrances on the way, is to be the priority of our lives. We are to become like Christ, and that will never happen if we leave our sin unattended and unchecked. This race is not intended for fun and games or for a Christian life of ease. It is for the prize, the upward call of Christ Jesus!

> *But one thing I do: forgetting what lies behind* [our sin] *and reaching forward to what lies ahead* [our holiness and God's constant presence], *I press on toward the goal for the prize of the upward call of God in Christ Jesus* (Philippians 3:13b-14).

You are nearing the end of this book, but the journey of the spiritual healing of your heart is just beginning. Our hearts, tattered and ripped by our sin and our stumbling blocks, are also divided by them. But we can still run with endurance the race of which every believer is a part: the race of holiness and Christlikeness as characterized by our surrender of the sin in our lives and by obedience to Christ, which replaces it. By enduring the race in this way, our hearts will be sewn up, and we will begin to see God *"unite* [our hearts] *to fear* [His] *name."* To have a united heart is the goal. It is the prize. It is our spiritual healing. And now it is time to tie on your running shoes! Ready, set, go!

INTROSPECTION

1. What are you doing practically to lay aside your "encumbrances and sin"? Are you using your heart diagram?

2. What impedes your walk that isn't specifically a sin?

3. What sin is satan using to attack you, seemingly from every direction, so that he can prevent you from finishing the race and being a positive influence on other believers?

4. What can you do to make a course correction and run the race well?

5. You have not yet endured like Jesus, to the point of death. But since He has, He is your example. Are you willing to make enduring the journey your life task?

ENDNOTES

1. Joseph M. Stowell, *Fan The Flame* (Chicago, IL: Moody Publishers, 1986), 32.

2. Zodhiates, *The Complete Word Study Dictionary: New Testament*, 240, #659.

3. Zodhiates, 1,025, #3591.

4. Zodhiates, 130, #266.

5. www. rjperalta.wordpress.com/category/disciples-of-christ/.

6. Zodhiates, *The Complete Word Study Dictionary* 680, #2139.

7. Zodhiates, *The Complete Word Study Dictionary* 1,394, #5143-I.

8. Zodhiates, *The Complete Word Study Dictionary* 1,425, #5281-II.

9. Zodhiates, *The Complete Word Study Dictionary* 78, #73.

10. Zodhiates, *The Complete Word Study Dictionary* 78, #73.

CHAPTER 12

UNITE MY HEART
TO FEAR YOUR NAME

Teach me Your way, O Lord; I will walk in Your truth; unite my heart to fear Your name (Psalm 86:11).

Have you heard the old adage, "You can lead a horse to water, but you can't make it drink"? Well, here is the real truth of that statement. You can't even lead a horse to water if he refuses to go. All you can do for some horses is say, "There's the water over there. If you want to drink, you will have to walk yourself there. I will come along for the journey if you'd like, but I'm not going to drag you there!" You have nearly completed this book. It has been full of information about your heart and how it can be, and should be, transformed. As you read this last chapter, my prayer is that you will look forward, see the "water," and go take a thirst-quenching drink, over and over.

REVIEWING THE JOURNEY

Throughout this book, you have been given three visual aids to help you grow in your understanding of what your heart truly looks like. We have examined the Tabernacle of the Old Testament in light of how it represents the journey of our hearts, our very lives, from the moment that we step "into" Christ to the moment that we are face to face with

Him in eternity. We have looked at a simple representation of our heart with all of its breaches and cracks, gaining a unique look at the sins, the gods, and the idols that have accumulated there since our birth. Finally, in the chapters on surrender, we were able to visualize how those layers of sin can trap the Holy Spirit inside of us unless we break through the sin with our surrender and repentance. I believe that these visuals will help us all see that the matter of our heart is serious business to God. He desires that our hearts be a proper home for Him, one in which He is comfortable.

Without an understanding that we are to enter into a relationship with Jesus so that we can begin to be conformed to His image, we will helplessly wander in the wilderness of salvation without sanctification. From our salvation to standing in the presence of the Living God, we are to be engaged in a progressive process that is designed to unite, bind up, and restore our broken and damaged hearts. This sanctification, our perfecting in Christ, is accomplished when we begin to surrender piece by painful piece to the only One who can transform our hearts into hearts that are united and that fear the name of Jesus. Do you see the incredible pictures that God has painted for our growth and healing in Him?

Out of God's great desire for us to walk in a deep and intimate relationship with Him where we begin to turn over our lives to His full control, He woos us by His Spirit to walk through the Door of Jesus. We are saved through our belief in Jesus when we walk through the Jesus Door. We then claim His sacrifice on the cross, at the bronze altar, as His act of personal sacrifice on our behalf, and we are baptized in the cleansing water found at the bronze laver whereby we associate ourselves with Jesus' death, burial, and resurrection. This is our Outer Court experience, but it is not the end. It is not the goal. It is not the place of greater intimacy.

As we continue to make our way through the Tabernacle, our journey takes us into the Inner Court. Do you remember? It is the place where we begin to grow up in our faith. It takes some (like me) many years to pass though that particular door because we are content with our Christian life, just the way it is. Others begin to grow right away, flourishing in the Holy Spirit, in the Word, and in pure worship to the Lord. No matter into which category you happen to fall, the Inner Court is a place where we go deeper with the Lord by way of walking in the Spirit, delving deeper into the Word, and learning to worship in both Spirit and truth found in the Word. Our growth is evidenced by our greater fruit. But this fruit is not limited to the ministry that God is doing through us. We must also focus on the fruit that is being borne out within us. Yes, the Inner Court is the place where we identify, confess, dispossess, and take full vengeance on those actions and attitudes that do not line up with the Word and the Spirit. It is also the place where we learn to follow the commands that are found in the Word. The door into the Inner Court is our crossroads. If we choose the path into the Inner Court, we will be aligned and adjusted in our hearts to the good and perfect will of God, and begin to obey His commands with our whole hearts.

A marvelous thing happens when we are consistently seeking to turn over our whole lives to the Lord Jesus Christ through our confession of sin and the surrender of our wills to His. Through deeper study, a closer walk with the Spirit, and worship from a more pure heart, we discover brief times of intimacy with the Lord such as we have never before experienced. These are indescribable moments of joy that only flow from a heart that is chasing after the God who can restore it. And ultimately, our earthly level of intimacy will grow exponentially when we see Him face to face in Heaven.

THE COURTS DEFINED

The Tabernacle is where we meet Jesus. It is where we identify our lives with His. It is where we give Him the rule of our broken lives, tarnished with sin. It is where our intimacy with Him grows. It is a picture of the journey of our heart.

Remind yourself now of the words and phrases we used earlier in the book to characterize each of the Tabernacle courts.

THE OUTER COURT	THE INNER COURT	THE HOLY OF HOLIES
Introduction to Christ	Illumination of Christ	Intimacy with Christ
Discipline (Decision)	Desire	Delight
Contrite (All Sin)	Change of Heart	Complete Heart
The Way	The Truth	The Life
No fruit or little fruit	More fruit	Much fruit
Belief	Adjustment (Individual Sin)	Obedience
Jesus	Spirit	Father
Gain the Name (Christian)	Gain Relationship	Gain God's continual presence
My Savior	My Lord/Master	My All/Ruler/King
Pardon	Purity	Paradise (rest)
Faith	Hope	Love (the greatest)

YOUR ACTIVE APPROACH

Look again at them. Are you in the same court as when you began to read this book, or have you covered some ground on your way into the next court? Which one is your current address? Each of the courts can be reached by taking appropriate steps, and sometimes even leaps, in our spiritual lives. The goal is always to reach the presence of God in the Holy of Holies. But your arrival there will depend on these two things: you and the choices you make! If you never choose to die to yourself and your sinful ways, you will never walk boldly into the Holy of Holies here on earth, for no flesh can reside in His presence. So to reach that goal, one must die to self. Do you remember that the placement of everything in the Tabernacle lines up into a cross? In order for Jesus to secure a way for us to travel through the Tabernacle into the presence of God, He had to sacrifice His life on a sinner's cross. If we desire to bask in His presence, we must choose to do the same. He died for our sinfulness, but our sin still is present in us to many varying degrees. His intimate presence will only be gained when we die to the sin still found in us. The Tabernacle was a prophetic picture of Christ's death. It was also a prophetic picture of what is required of us; it shows us how we must die as well.

Theory must always give way to practical application, or else all of our "head knowledge" becomes wasted and worthless grey matter. Can we focus in for just a little while on the Inner Court, the place of our heart transformation? Let's magnify it right now so that we can't see our beginning or our end, just the present, the here and now.

It is in the Inner Court where God allows us to see just how dark and sinful our hearts are and can be. It is a place of illumination. Once in the Inner Court, once we have taken a "look around" at our hearts, we often find that the sins, the gods, and the idols we find there are overwhelming to us. We know that we are to be about building our hearts into a proper and clean home for the Lord, sweeping out all that He would not enjoy. Just like the Israelites of Haggai's day that we looked at in Chapter 6, we know that we are to "rebuild" our hearts, which is the temple/Tabernacle of God. But we respond just like they did, don't we?

We follow after our own priorities, and we leave our hearts in desolation and destruction while living flesh-influenced lives. Our breaches, fractures, and sin remain, and our lives do not even remotely resemble that of Christ's! We continue going on our merry way, prioritizing everything else in life except our walk with Jesus toward a holy life. And just like the Israelites, our wrong priorities lead to consequences, and some are severe. Our lives become fruitless, barren, and deserted. This reveals that our hearts have not been transformed by intimacy with Christ. Joanna Weaver relates to this personally. She saw it and experienced it like this:

> It is not enough simply to be associated. To be acquainted. We
> have to be spiritually grafted on—to draw our life from him, to

be so closely attached that we would wither and die if we were cut off.

I missed that point for a long time. I had spent so much of my life concentrating on the "fruit" of my own personal holiness, that I missed out on the connection, the sweet intimacy of being attached to the Vine. And as a result, what I tried to do was as ludicrous as an apple tree branch trying to produce apples by its own effort.

"Be good, be good. Do good, do good," the broken branch chants as it lies on the orchard grass. "That apple should be popping out anytime," says the helpless, lifeless stick.

But that is not how it works. It's the tree, not the branch that determines the fruit. The tree is the life source. The branch has no power of its own. But once it gets connected, once that sap gets flowing and those leaves start growing, that insignificant little twig will find itself loaded with fruit. And it didn't have to do anything—except abide.[1]

Our lesson from these Israelites is that hard work will be required of us to rebuild our hearts and bring them under Christ's full control. But the hard work of learning how to walk by the Spirit, make the Word our life's roadmap, and worship as God desires will reveal to God and others something of great significance—our obedience.

Everyone's heart is in some form of disrepair. It is our individual responsibility to do the hard work of the Inner Court experience in order to show that we have our priorities right and that we desire to be obedient to God's call into His presence. This pleases and glorifies God, just as when the remnant went to the mountain to gather wood for the rebuilding of the temple.

Once we have attacked our own wrong priorities by obeying God's command to rebuild our hearts, we can begin to seek the Spirit so that we might know what gods, idols, and sins are in our hearts. Ironically, it is these dark places in our hearts that often keep us from right priorities. For example, the sin of investing too much time in front of the television will often be the reason that we are not spending much time with God.

God is a patient God. He never required us to "get clean" before we could be His children. Jesus' sacrifice was enough for us to join His family. However, He patiently waits for us to come before Him with each thing that separates us from intimacy with Him. What He has graciously and patiently let remain in us may now be the very idol or sin that He requires us to sacrifice today. God is a patient God, but He will not be patient forever when it comes to our sin. His desire is for it to be rooted out of us. He wants to be the only God that we worship, serve, and bow down to. He will settle for nothing less.

How did you do with the soul-searching assignment in Chapter 6? Did you fill in the heart with your now illuminated, identified, and magnified sin? Did God reveal to you some things in your heart that you didn't even know were there? Have you begun to keep charge of your heart by confessing these gods and sins to the Lord and have you been praying consistently for Him to transform these areas of your heart? Do you realize that once He has transformed each part that He showed you, it will be time to create a new heart, and this will continue for the rest of your life? Have you completed the assignment? Have you shared your testimony with anyone? This is taking full vengeance on your enemies! This is the hard work of the Inner Court.

With our gods and sins exposed, with our minds now set on their removal from our hearts, and with our prayers reaching the heavens for God to take control of these areas, we begin to see just how important this process is to God. Our sins are the very walls that separate us from intimacy with Him. Sin makes God's children impure, unholy, and no longer set apart for Him. To spare any of our sins for our own benefit breaks the heart of God. In sparing the gods of our own hearts, we hinder, and even threaten, a deep and intimate relationship with God, and we stay in a constant "sin-confess-sin-confess" lifestyle. We are not living authentic Christian lives when we try to keep alive the sins that will destroy us. These sins that we ignore, and thus spare, will have devastating effects on our walk, our witness, and our ministry.

Obedience is required in order for us to fully put to death our gods and sins. Without our fully following God's commands, we will never kill those things that can kill us spiritually, and possibly even physically. If we really want to attempt full obedience to the Word, we will have to get to the place where we are confessing our sins as they come to our attention. We can no longer allow them to slide by for the moment while giving God our, "I'm sorry." God isn't as interested in our apologies as He is in our brokenness and true repentance of the heart. If we do not grasp the severity of our willful disobedience and how much it hurts God's heart, we will never see the need to turn away from those sins. Instead, we will return over and over to our idol worship.

If you choose to continue in sin, you must remember that God will let your sin find you out! In case you have never been there, removing sin from your life as the Spirit reveals it is far easier than having to remove sin that you have been caught in! Humiliation is a tough teacher, but she is effective! That is what makes our surrender key in dispossessing everything that trips us up. And remember, surrender is not waving the white flag to the enemy. It is giving ourselves up totally to the power and control of the God who loves us with great passion. Let these definitions guide you in your own surrender. Surrender is choosing to:

- Walk in the Spirit instead of in your own flesh.

- Die to your self and become a new creation.

- Worship God through love and sacrifice and obedience.

- Be humble before God in order to pray to Him, seek His face, and turn from the things that you do that are evil in His sight.

- Allow your flesh to be crucified and die every day so that you can walk through the veil and into His glorious presence.

- Focus on God's will as your priority instead of what your flesh desires.

- Be broken by God for sin you have left unattended for too long.

- Be willing to make a 180-degree turn in an action, thought, or word.

- Be open to the Spirit taking control so He can gush out of you.

- Die for the glory of God!

GOD'S TRANSFORMING POWER THROUGH SURRENDER

Now that we have reached the end of this journey, I must share something that the Lord shared with me as I was completing this book. For quite a while now, I have believed that a heart can never be transformed by an act of our will, mostly because our will resides in our flesh, and that flesh is ever decaying and can never be improved. I believe that, in the same way that we may not be saved without an act of God's will, we cannot be sanctified and transformed without the same kind of act of God's will. When God transforms my heart, then my actions follow. If I choose to act out of my flesh, as I have when I have made New Year's resolutions, it is possible that I might get some results to begin with, but they are always short-lived. I am capable of changing some things for a period of time, but only God can change my heart. When God is given the opportunity to work out His will in my heart and life through my surrender and obedience to Him, there is a lasting, even eternal, transformation that takes place in me.

But there is an act of my will that God requires of me. God is looking into hearts, not to see if we will stop a particular sin. He is watching to see if our will simply desires to line up with His. The specifics of our sin are less important than the act of our will that wants to obey in child-like faith.

Our obedience is seen when we are faithful to ask the Spirit to reveal our sin. Our obedience is seen when we are faithful to confess what is revealed to us as sin that displeases God. Our obedience is seen when we are faithful to place that sin under His control so that He might be Lord over it. This is the obedience that He requires of us, and, He is the only one who is capable of transforming the heart that is surrendered to Him.

When the sin is put in His hands to deal with, God will then, by His Spirit, give some directives for our obedient hearts to follow, things to do in response to His Lordship over the issue. When I choose to follow the directive with a still-surrendered heart, heart change will occur. It will always be about the Spirit's work in us, not an act of human will. Oswald Chambers said it like this in *My Utmost for His Highest*:

> So often we mar God's designed influence through us by our self-conscious effort to be consistent and useful. Jesus says that there is only one way to develop spiritually, and that is by concentration on God . . . pay attention to the Source, and out of you will flow rivers of living water. We cannot get at the springs of our natural life by common sense.[2]

The problem is that we get this all backward, and then we wonder why we never gain victory over our sins. We think that we grow when we set out to do what we "ought," and not do what we think we "ought not."

As God was revealing this through a couple of devotionals not long ago, He knew that He had prepared an extra special treat for me in my personal Bible study. That morning I was reading in Zechariah 3–4, and my eyes came across this very familiar verse, and it took on a new and fresh meaning. God's revelation to me was so awesome!

This is the word of the Lord to Zerubbabel saying, "Not by might nor by power, but by My Spirit," says the Lord of hosts (Zechariah 4:6).

Now this was a word to Zerubbabel from God through Zechariah, and He was referring to how Zerubbabel was to finish the temple—neither by his own might nor by his own strength. God's Word to Zerubbabel was that that temple would only be completed by the Spirit! Did you get that? The temple, the house of God, is our hearts! How will we complete and perfect our own hearts? Not by our fleshly might or power! We will see our hearts perfected and made holy by the Spirit alone! Our hearts are the home of the Living God, and they need to be built up appropriately so that He is comfortable living there. Our hearts are to be built up according to God's perfect design in accordance with His whole Word. How could we ever possibly get that done? The only way to repair, and thus complete, our hearts is by the Spirit. There is no other way. Not by our might nor by our power, but by the Spirit my heart and yours will be transformed into a wonderful home for God, if we will but surrender to His work in us.

Wow! The burden to build the temple of my heart was never meant to rest on my shoulders. But it will be brought to completion as I realize my daily sins, confess them, surrender to God, and obey whatever God tells me to do after that! God's Spirit will complete the good work that He has begun in me! Let this revelation minister to you and defeat the lie that it is up to you to change your own heart. Be set free from striving to repair your broken, fragmented, and sin-ridden heart, as I have been! It is God alone who will restore your heart, the Tabernacle of God! Warren Wiersbe summed it up this way:

> Hudson Taylor had definite convictions about how God's work should be done. We can make our best plans and try to carry them out in our own strength. Or we can make careful plans and ask God to bless them. "Yet another way of working is to begin with God; to ask His plans, and to offer ourselves to Him to carry out His purposes."[3]

This now is my prayer for you as you continue on in the process of having your heart, God's Tabernacle, spiritually healed, from divided between flesh and Spirit, from broken to restored:

> *I pray that the eyes of your heart may be enlightened, so that you will know what is the hope of His calling, what are the riches of the glory of His inheritance in the saints, and what is the surpassing greatness of His power toward us who believe. These are in accordance with the working of the strength of His might which He brought about in Christ, when He raised Him from the dead and seated Him at His right hand in the heavenly places....* (Ephesians 1:18-20).

Continue on, dear brothers and sisters! Fix your eyes on the Holy of Holies while you walk through the chambers of the Tabernacle of your heart and journey. Keep moving, never stopping, until you reach the goal, the glorious presence of our Father in Heaven. O God, unite the hearts of all Your children and restore them, that we might fear Your name! By this may You be glorified forever and ever. Amen!

INTROSPECTION

1. Look back at the Tabernacle. Review its courts and the furnishings. Review the word chart. Could you now communicate to another believer that it is God's design for us to walk through the entire Tabernacle, what are the typical actions of a believer in each of the courts, that it is the entire journey that will make a restored heart possible, and that this journey will lead to deeper intimacy with God? Use this as a tool to help someone else in his or her journey.

2. Look at the Tabernacle again. Are you in the same court as when you started? Are you closer to the next door you are to enter?

3. If you filled in the heart diagram, do you see the Holy Spirit making progress as He restores your broken heart? If so, continue laying it before Him. When you fill it all up with highlighter, begin another heart and repeat the process. If you do not see progress, you might return to the assignment and begin again. Do not lose heart. As you are faithful, God will be faithful! Share this diagram with just one other person, and be accountable with him or her. Everyone needs a friend as they lay down their sins.

4. Are you setting your mind on repentance, surrender, and obedience? These are the acts of turning around, laying down your "rights," and following Jesus.

5. Look at the artesian well diagram. Is this a picture of the Holy Spirit being unleashed in and through you? It is by your brokenness and surrender that you allow Jesus to live His life through you. There is great power in surrender, and Jesus wants that power to be at work in your life that others might be drawn to Him.

ENDNOTES

1. Joanna Weaver, *Having a Mary Heart in a Martha World* (Colorado Springs, CO: Waterbrook Press, 2002), 76-77.

2. Oswald Chambers, *My Utmost for His Highest* (Grand Rapids, MI: Discovery House Publishers, 1963), 139.

3. Warren Wiersbe, *Wycliffe Handbook of Preaching and Preachers* (Chicago, IL: Moody Press, 1984), 243, www.sermonillustrations.com/a-z/p/planning.htm.

APPENDIX A

SCRIPTURAL SUPPORT
OF THE COMPARISON OF
THE TABERNACLE TO
A BELIEVER'S HEART JOURNEY

THE TABERNACLE, OUR HEART

*For this reason I bow my knees before the Father . . . that He would grant you, according to the riches of His glory, to be strengthened with power through His Spirit **in the inner man**, so that Christ may dwell in your **hearts** through faith . . . that you may be **filled up to all the fullness of God*** (Ephesians 3:14-19).

THE DOOR, JESUS

I am the door; if anyone enters through Me, he will be saved, and will go in and out and find pasture (John 10:9).

THE ALTAR, OUR SALVATION BASED
ON THE SACRIFICE OF JESUS ON THE CROSS

Then came the first day of Unleavened Bread on which the Passover lamb had to be sacrificed.

When they came to the place called The Skull, there they crucified Him and the criminals, one on the right and the other on the left (Luke 22:7; 23:33).

THE LAVER, OUR BAPTISM

...Having been buried with Him in baptism, in which you were also raised up with Him through faith in the working of God, who raised Him from the dead (Colossians 2:12).

THE LAMP STAND, THE HOLY SPIRIT

But when He, the Spirit of truth, comes, He will guide you into all the truth (John 16:13a).

...But just as it is written, "Things which eye has not seen and ear has not heart, and which have not entered the heart of man, all that God has prepared for the those who love Him." For to us God revealed them through the Spirit; for the Spirit searches all things, even the depths of God (I Corinthians 2:9-10).

THE TABLE OF SHOWBREAD, THE WORD

He humbled you and let you be hungry, and fed you with manna which you did not know, nor did your fathers know, that He might make you understand that man does not live by bread alone, but man lives by everything that proceeds out of the mouth of the Lord (Deuteronomy 8:3).

Give us this day our daily bread (Matthew 6:11).

THE ALTAR OF INCENSE, OUR TRUE WORSHIP

The sons of Amram were Aaron and Moses. And Aaron was set apart to sanctify him as most holy, he and his sons forever, to burn incense before the Lord, to minister to Him and to bless in His name forever (I Chronicles 23:13).

But an hour is coming, and now is, when the true worshipers will worship the Father in spirit and truth; for such people the Father seeks to be His worshipers (John 4:23).

Therefore I urge you, brethren, by the mercies of God, to present your bodies a living and holy sacrifice, acceptable to God, which is your spiritual service of worship (Romans 12:1).

The Veil, our flesh

> *And behold, the veil of the temple was torn in two from top to bottom; and the earth shook and the rocks were split* (Matthew 27:51).

> *Therefore, brethren, since we have confidence to enter the holy place by the blood of Jesus, by a new and living way which He inaugurated for us through the veil, that is, His flesh....* (Hebrews 10:19-20).

> *Now those who belong to Christ Jesus have crucified the flesh with its passions and desires* (Galatians 5:24).

The Ark of the Covenant and Mercy Seat, God's abiding presence within us

> *You shall put this altar in front of the veil that is near the ark of the testimony, in front of the mercy seat that is over the ark of the testimony, where I will meet with you* (Exodus 30:6).

> *"...and they shall call His name Immanuel," which translated means, "God with us"* (Matthew 1:23).

> *... and lo, I am with you always, even to the end of the age* (Matthew 28:19-20).

> *...for through Him we both have our access in one Spirit to the Father. So then you are no longer strangers and aliens, but you are fellow citizens with the saints, and are of God's household, having been built on the foundation of the apostles and prophets, Christ Jesus Himself being the corner stone, in whom the whole building, being fitted together, is growing into a holy temple in the Lord, in whom you also are being built together into a dwelling of God in the Spirit* (Ephesians 2:18-22).

APPENDIX B

DETERMINING WHERE YOU STAND IN THE TABERNACLE

THE OUTER COURT	THE INNER COURT	THE HOLY OF HOLIES
Introduction	Illumination	Intimacy
Discipline or Decision (Door)	Desire	Delight
Contrite Heart (Repentance of the totality of our sin)	Change of Heart	Complete Heart
The Way	The Truth	The Life
No fruit or little fruit	More fruit	Much fruit
Justification	Sanctification	Glorification
Belief	Adjustment (Repentance of our individual daily sin)	Full Obedience
Jesus	Holy Spirit	Father
Gain the Name (Christian)	Gain the Relationship	Gain God's continual Presence

cont.

THE OUTER COURT	THE INNER COURT	THE HOLY OF HOLIES
My Savior	My Lord/Master	My All/Ruler/King
Pardon	Purity	Paradise (rest)
Faith	Hope	Love (the greatest)

ABOUT CHERYL GNAGEY

You have been on a long and sometimes difficult journey, one that will continue on until you go home to meet your Lord and Savior. God's perfect plan for your walk is to bring you in and take you through the courts of His Tabernacle, all the way into the Holy of Holies. As you have read through this book, you have been challenged to know exactly where you are in that journey, to understand what is preventing you from walking forward, and to surrender to God in such a way that you experience victory in your walk.

It is my hope and prayer that as you have read through *Spiritual Healing*, your heart has been, and will continue to be, radically transformed—that you are experiencing your own spiritual healing! If that describes you, and *Spiritual Healing* has had an impact on your life, I would love to hear about it and will pray for your continued growth! If you have had a transformation that you would like to share with me, I would be thrilled to receive your testimony or an invitation to speak at your church at: cherylgnagey@gmail.com

If you would like to view my speaking schedule, visit my Website at:

www.cherylgnagey.com

www.cherylgnagey.blogspot.com

It has been a pleasure traveling the Highway to Holiness with you. As we now part ways, continue to follow the path set before you. I will as well, and we will surely meet again!

. . . We have not ceased to pray for you and to ask that you may be filled with the knowledge of His will in all spiritual wisdom and understanding, so that you will walk in a manner worthy of the Lord, to please Him in all respects, bearing fruit in every good work and increasing in the knowledge of God; strengthened with all power, according to His glorious might, for the attaining of all steadfastness and patience; joyously giving thanks to the Father, who has qualified us to share in the inheritance of the saints in Light (Colossians 1:9-12).

IN THE RIGHT HANDS, THIS BOOK WILL CHANGE LIVES!

Most of the people who need this message will not be looking for this book. To change their lives, you need to put a copy of this book in their hands.

> *But others (seeds) fell into good ground, and brought forth fruit, some a hundred-fold, some sixty-fold, some thirty-fold* (Matthew 13:8).

Our ministry is constantly seeking methods to find the good ground, the people who need this anointed message to change their lives. Will you help us reach these people?

> *Remember this—a farmer who plants only a few seeds will get a small crop. But the one who plants generously will get a generous crop* (2 Corinthians 9:6).

EXTEND THIS MINISTRY BY SOWING
3 BOOKS, 5 BOOKS, 10 BOOKS, OR MORE TODAY,
AND BECOME A LIFE CHANGER!

Thank you,

Don Nori Sr., Founder
Destiny Image
Since 1982

DESTINY IMAGE PUBLISHERS, INC.

*"Speaking to the Purposes of God for This Generation
and for the Generations to Come."*

VISIT OUR NEW SITE HOME AT
WWW.DESTINYIMAGE.COM

FREE SUBSCRIPTION TO DI NEWSLETTER

Receive free unpublished articles by top DI authors, exclusive

discounts, and free downloads from our best and newest books.

Visit www.destinyimage.com to subscribe.

Write to: Destiny Image
              P.O. Box 310
              Shippensburg, PA 17257-0310

Call: 1-800-722-6774

Email: orders@destinyimage.com

For a complete list of our titles or to place an order
online, visit www.destinyimage.com.

FIND US ON FACEBOOK OR FOLLOW US ON TWITTER.

www.facebook.com/destinyimage   facebook
www.twitter.com/destinyimage   twitter